WE BELIEVE IN GOD

WE BELIEVE IN GOD

WILLIAM BARCLAY   ANTHONY BLOOM
COLIN BROWN   ELSIE CHAMBERLAIN
THOMAS CORBISHLEY   RUPERT E. DAVIES
W. DONALD HUDSON   JOHN LAWRENCE
HYWEL D. LEWIS   HAROLD LOUKES
PAULINE M. WEBB

Edited with an Introduction by
RUPERT E. DAVIES

London
GEORGE ALLEN AND UNWIN LTD
RUSKIN HOUSE MUSEUM STREET

PRINTED IN GREAT BRITAIN
in 11 point Plantin type
BY WILLMER BROTHERS LIMITED
BIRKENHEAD

FOREWORD

It is sometimes put about that belief in God is a discredited superstition which is maintained only by the ill-informed and the eccentric. Here are eleven men and women, neither ill-informed nor eccentric, members of various Christian denominations but in no sense writing as official spokesmen, who are prepared to set down frankly their belief in God and their reasons for it. It may be that their testimony and their arguments will confirm the faith of some and disturb the doubts of others.

I am extremely grateful to Mr Philip Unwin for promoting and encouraging the project.

RUPERT E. DAVIES

Bristol, June 1967

CONTENTS

WILLIAM BARCLAY

was born in Wick, Caithness, in 1907, and educated at Dalziel High School, Motherwell, and the Universities of Glasgow and Marburg. He obtained an M.A. with First Class Honours in Classics and a B.D. with distinction in the New Testament, and is an Honorary D.D. of Edinburgh. He has been Bruce Lecturer, Kerr Lecturer and Croall Lecturer. He was Minister of Trinity Church, Renfrew, from 1933 to 1947, Lecturer in New Testament and Hellenistic Greek at Glasgow University from 1947 to 1963, and since then has been Professor of Divinity and Biblical Criticism in that University. He is married with one son and one daughter. He is the author of more than fifty books, of which The Daily Study Bible *is probably the best known.*

WILLIAM BARCLAY

I believe in God – it would be odd if I didn't. I was brought up
in a Christian home. My father was a bank manager, but he was
an elder of the Church, and, layman as he was, he had preached
in almost every pulpit in Motherwell, where I was brought up.
My mother was the nearest approach to a saint that I have ever
met in this world. My early days were centred on the Church. It
was not that I was in any way specially or precociously religious.
It was simply that for sport and for pleasure and even for parties
and dancing I turned to the church premises. I was in the Boys'
Brigade, and it was there that I went for football and swimming
and camping. My school was Dalziel High School, with its morning assembly at which the senior pupils read the Bible lesson, and
sometimes even took the prayers. The first time I ever spoke in
public, or conducted a religious meeting, was in Motherwell
YMCA, and the first time I ever appeared in print was in the
YMCA magazine. When I went to Glasgow University in 1929
A. A. Bowman, the then professor of Moral Philosophy, was a
strong Christian force. I was a classicist and John Swinnerton
Phillimore was one of the greatest teachers of his day, and a devout Roman Catholic. The result of all this was that I was brought
up in an atmosphere of religion. It was not an atmosphere of piety;
it was not that religion was what today young people call 'holy';
it was not the kind of situation in which we went to evangelical
rallies, or walked about carrying a Bible, or stood up and confessed our faith. It was simply that the Church and all that it
stood for was a natural and healthy way of life.

In 1929 I began the study of divinity in what was then Trinity
College, Glasgow. For most young men that is a difficult time.
Their beliefs are challenged and sometimes shattered. The actions
of 'the acids of modernity' become evident in the critical approach
to scripture, and sometimes an older faith has to be surrendered

before a new faith can be found. I too could say what Lord
Hermand said to the General Assembly of the Church of Scotland
in 1805: 'Sir! I sucked in the being and attributes of God with
my mother's milk.' But my experience in the school of divinity
was not like that. The new approach did not worry me. I was a
classicist by trade, and I approached the biblical books and history
and theology very much as I had previously approached classical
texts. I found it far more interesting than disturbing. And that
was so, as I can see when I look back, because the whole matter
was still external to me. I was still detached from it. Religion and
the Church were part of the happy background of life, but even
yet they had not arrived in the foreground for anything like de-
liberate committal to them.

I think that another factor has to be brought into the situation.
I think that belief is easier for some people than for others. It is
not a matter of life being easier for some people than for others.
It is not that a trouble-free life begets belief or that desolating
experience begets unbelief. It is not a matter of great mental
power. It is not that great mental power produces unbelief or that
simplicity begets belief. It is a matter of what we can only call
temperament. There are some who have a believing temperament
and some who have not. To some belief is effortless and natural, to
others it is strange and difficult. I think that I happen to have this
believing temperament. It is not that life has been easy for me
and that the wind has never blown on me. I saw my mother
die with agonizing cancer of the spine. We lost a daughter when
life was opening out to her. I myself have had for forty years
to face the handicap of severe deafness. And yet I have never found
belief difficult. This is not to say that I have never had a doubt or
a questioning or a sense of forsakenness. But it is to say that
even then there was a kind of basic belief in God. This is not a
matter which can be set down to anyone's credit. It is a thing
which is, or is not, a built-in matter of temperament, a part of
oneself. George Bernard Shaw more than once told of an experience he claimed to have had. He found himself in a vegetarian
restaurant in the Barbican, sitting opposite a man who began to
discuss religion with him. 'I can see,' said this man, 'that you are
a sceptic.' 'How do you know?' Shaw asked. 'I am a bit of a
phrenologist,' the man said. 'Oh,' said Shaw, 'have I no bump of

12

veneration?' 'Bump of veneration!' the man said. 'Why, it's a hole.' A man is born a natural sceptic or a natural believer. And I think that I was born with this built-in inclination towards belief.

I believe in God – but this is an affirmation of belief which has to have much more definition than mere statement. *What kind of God?* is the all-important question.

In the Old Testament story of the messenger from heaven who came to Manoah to tell him that a son was to be born to him there is the incident in which Manoah discovers who his heavenly visitor was, and says to his wife 'We shall surely die, for we have seen God' (Judges 13:22). Do I believe in a God whom it is death to see?

Job chapters 38 and 39 are perhaps the most tremendous poetry in the Bible. They are the answer of God to Job. 'Where were you when I laid the foundations of the earth? ... Have you entered into the springs of the sea? ... Have you entered the store-houses of the snow? ... Can you bind the chains of the Pleiades?' Again and again the God of this great drama hurls his artillery of unanswerable questions against the defenceless head of Job. And the whole essence of this divine barrage is: 'Who are you to speak to me? What right have you to talk to me?' Do I believe in a God before whom I can only bow in broken submission?

The Stoics had their strange view of God. They insisted that the first and essential characteristic and attribute of God is *apatheia*. *Apatheia* in Greek does not mean *apathy* in English. Apathy in English is indifference, which might have been and could be, otherwise. *Apatheia* is essential incapability of all feeling. The argument was that if God can feel any emotion, then a man can make God sad or make God glad. But to be able to change a person's emotion is at least for the moment to have some power over that person. No one, so they argued, can have any power over God, for, if he had, he would be for that moment greater than God. Therefore God must be essentially insulated from all feelings and emotion; he must be *apathés*, incapable of feeling. Do I believe in a God, who for the very reason that he is God, cannot and must not care?

The Epicureans had their gods. For the Epicurean the one good in life was serenity. So the Epicurean gods lay beside their nectar in their golden houses out in the *intermundia,* the spaces between the worlds, and were not even aware of the sinking ships and the clanging fights and the praying hands of men in the world below. Do I believe in a God or in gods whose only wish is their own serenity and who, however much I care for them, are even unaware that I exist?

Is it enough for me to agree, at least provisionally, that the working hypothesis of God is as good an explanation of the world as any? Is it enough for me to look at the order of the world and to say that there must be a God, and that that God must be, as Jeans said, a mathematician? Can I too, again thinking of the order of the world, say: 'No astronomer can be an atheist'? It is true that the argument from the world to God still seems to me, who am neither theologian nor philosopher, persuasive. Long ago the Stoics said that you might as well hope to put the letters of the alphabet in large quantities into a bucket, and pour them out, and have them fall into the plays of Ennius, as to explain a world without God. A house, said Cicero, implies an architect and a builder. So does a world. A man can make an orrery, a working-scale model of the planets. If it takes a man to make the model, did the original come into existence by sheer chance?

I am old-fashioned and simple enough still to be impressed by Paley's analogy. A man is walking across a moor and finds a watch. He has never in his life before seen a watch and he does not know what it is. He examines it. He finds it a complicated arrangement of jewels and levers and springs and cogged wheels, all ticking away, with a case of gold and a face of porcelain. Further examination shows him that the hands are moving round the dial in what is clearly a predetermined order. Does he then say: 'By chance all these things came together from the ends of the earth and formed themselves into a watch; by chance they wound themselves up and set themselves going; by chance they move in an ordered way'? No. His argument will almost certainly be: 'I have found a watch. *Somewhere there must be a watch-maker.*' So we find a world more accurate than any watch. Order implies mind. Somewhere there must be a world-maker.

I am well aware that Apaley's argument is out of date. And I am also well aware that, if it did prove anything, it would rather prove that once there had been a watch-maker, not that a watch-maker still does exist. But, even if I do accept this argument, do I believe in a God who is a worldmaker?

Do I believe in a God who is a puppet-master or worse? Thomas Hardy spoke of 'the dreaming, dark, dumb thing that turns the handle of the idle show'. Shelley called God 'the Almighty Fiend'. Swinburne in that grim passage in *Atalanta in Corydon* writes of God:

> The lord of love, of loathing and of strife,
>   Who gives a star and takes a sun away;
> Who shapes the soul, and makes her a barren wife
>   To the earthy body and grievous growth of clay;
> Who turns the large limbs to a little flame
>   And binds the great sea with a little sand;
> Who makes desire, and slays desire with shame;
>   Who shakes the heaven as ashes in his hand;
> Who seeing the light and shadow for the same,
>   Bids days waste night as fire devours a brand,
> Smites without sword and scourges without rod;
>   The supreme evil, God.

Do I believe in a God who is not the lover but the enemy of man?

Do I believe in a God who is a kind of Life Force or Creative Energy? In a once famous poem William Herbert Caruth wrote:

> A fire mist, and a planet
>   A crystal and a cell,
> A jellyfish and a saurian,
>   And a cave where the cave-men dwell.
> Then a sense of law and beauty
>   And a face turned from the clod,
> Some call it Evolution,
>   Others call it God.

George Bernard Shaw gave a peculiar twist to this idea of God as the Life Force. His idea is the idea of an experimentalist God. The Life Force proceeds, as Shaw sees it, by trial and error. He has an essay on what he calls *The Infancy of God*. As Shaw sees it, we have a paradox in regard to God. God is the God of honour, of love, and of light. Yet at the same time God is the God of epilepsy, of cancer, of smallpox, of madness, of war, of poverty, of tyranny. Now, if we conceive of God as perfect and omnipotent, we get an intolerable situation, for we have to make God responsible for that which perfect omnipotence could never allow. Shaw therefore sees God as an experimentalist, in his infancy, as it were, with the further idea that, since God depends on men to carry out his experiments, he also depends on men to clear up the experiments that go wrong. So in *The Shewing-up of Blanco Posnet* he makes Blanco say about the baby with the croup: 'It was early days when He made the croup, I guess. It was the best He could think of then; but when it turned out wrong on His hands, He made you and me to fight the croup for Him. You bet He didn't make us for nothing; and He wouldn't have made us at all if He could have done His work without us. By Gum, that must be what we're for!' Do I then believe in a God who depends on me even more than I depend on him, an experimentalist Life Force, sharing his experiments with men?

It would, I think, be true to say that all these ideas of God, with the exception of those which think in terms of an utterly indifferent or an actively hostile God, have in them something of the God in whom I believe – but not everything, and not the most important things of all.

To arrive at what I believe about God, or rather, to arrive at the God in whom I believe, I must start again, and I must ask a question which is obviously of the first importance – What do I mean by this word *believe*?

There are clearly two kinds of belief. There is belief which is purely intellectual, but which has no total effect on life. There are many things of the truth of which I have no doubt; but they make no practical difference to my life and living. There are certain other things – they are naturally much fewer – which I not only believe with my mind, but which dominate my living. I am not only convinced of their theoretical truth, I am also convinced of what I might call their practical truth. John's Gospel speaks about *doing* the truth (John 3:21). There is a truth which I do, and a truth which I know.

In itself this is not a theological matter at all; it is simply a matter of life. I believe that the square on the hypotenuse of a right-angled triangle equals the sum of the squares on the other two sides. There are doubtless people for whom that fact is practically important, but it is not important to me. It makes no difference to my life and conduct. On the other hand, I believe that six and six make twelve, and I shall therefore resolutely refuse to pay one shilling and two pence for two sixpenny articles. Here is a belief which dominates my every action in life.

Now, when religion speaks about believing in God, it is the second kind of belief that it means. It does not mean simply an intellectual acceptance of the fact that there is a God; it means that, because I believe in God, my whole life is affected in its every area and in its every action. The writer of the Letter to the Hebrews drew just this distinction, when he said that 'whoever would draw near to God must believe that he exists and that he rewards those who seek him' (Hebrews II:6). Belief must mean not only belief in the existence of God, but belief in the impact of God upon life. When I use the word believe in connection with God, I do not mean simply intellectual belief, although that enters into it; I mean total belief, belief to which I am committed in action.

This might be put in another way which will involve the discussion of the meaning of another kindred word. What this really means is that I am convinced, not only that I am interested in God, but also that God is interested in me. We might almost say that it means, not only that I believe in God, but that God also believes in me. There is more than one way in which we can use the word *know*. There are clearly gradations in knowing, when the word is applied to persons. I may know a man by sight; I may know him to smile to; I may know him to pass the time of day to in my club. But there is a vast difference between my knowledge of this man and my knowledge of a life-long friend or of my wife. This is to say that into the word *know* something personal comes. There is all the difference in the world between *knowing about* a person and *knowing* a person. Knowing a person involves a personal relationship with that person. This personal element in knowledge is characteristic of the Bible. Hebrew, for instance, uses the word *know* of sexual intercourse. Adam knew Eve (Genesis 4:1). It is thus used of the most intimate and personal knowledge that one person can have of another. It is this personal kind of knowledge that the Bible means when it talks about knowing God. This is not knowing a theory, or a fact, or a theology; it is knowing a person. And that is precisely why there is nowhere in the Bible any proof or even attempted proof of the existence of God. The knowledge of God and his existence was not something which came by mental or intellectual activity as one kind of knowledge comes; it was knowledge which came from personal experience. I suppose that one might say of this kind of knowledge that, to arrive at it, the knowledge of the mind must turn into the knowledge of the heart. Detached knowing about must become intimate knowing.

So then when I speak about believing in God, I speak about a belief which does not remain an intellectual thing, but which becomes a thing of the total personality; and this believing must come from a knowing which is the result, not only of strenuous mental activity, but of intimate personal experience.

The argument is so far clear, and the need is so far clear, but, when we have taken the matter this length, there emerges the fact which cuts across the whole issue. *What I want appears to be impossible.* By definition, God is the infinite and I am the finite; God is the Creator and I am the created. It is impossible for the finite to know the infinite, and for the creature to know the Creator. If it was possible for man to know God, then God would simply be a kind of outsize man. So, then, we are led to two further conclusions.

First, if God is to be known in any real sense of the term, if God is to be known in this personal way, God must reveal himself. Such knowledge cannot be got by man climbing up; it must be got by God coming down. It cannot be got by man seeking. 'Can you find out the deep things of God? Can you find out the limit of the Almighty?' (Job 11:7, RSV), or, as the AV has it: 'Canst thou by searching find out God?' It must be got by God giving. It is true that the giving will be given to him who seeks, and that the revealing will come to the mind which searches. It is also true that, since any workman is known in his works, there are things which can be learned about the Creator from his creation. But even so, the personal knowledge cannot come by seeking and deduction. It must be given by God.

Second, even if this revelation is given, it cannot be the revelation of the whole of God. This is obviously something which no human mind can receive. The omnipotence, the omnipresence, the omniscience of God are not things which any mind can grasp. Deity cannot be comprehended in humanity, or it would cease to be Deity. A totally knowable and comprehensible God would not be God at all. God is of necessity beyond man. But there is something which can be known, if God chooses to make it known. *I can know the attitude of God to men and, therefore, the attitude of God to me.* And this personal knowledge is what matters. There are many things that a little child does not know or understand about his father, but he does know and understand his father's attitude to him, how his father feels about him. There are still more things that my dog does not understand and know about me, but he does know how I feel about him.

This is exactly what the Christian claims to know. It is the Christian claim that in Jesus of Nazareth we see fully displayed the attitude of God to men. I know that this statement is a statement of faith. It is not susceptible of proof. This is the leap of faith. Lyn Irvine in her book *Alison Cairns and her Family* says: 'We may have no argument and yet take a stand with the old woman who silenced Darwin's father. "Doctor, I know that sugar is sweet, and I know that my redeemer liveth".' It is the Christian affirmation of faith that in this Jesus we see the attitude of God to men. I would not claim that in Jesus we see the whole of God. We clearly do not see the omnipotence and the omniscience and the omnipresence of God in the earthly Jesus. According to the John of the Fourth Gospel Jesus said: 'He who has seen me has seen' – what or whom? Not God, but *the Father.* It is the attitude of God towards men that we see in Jesus, so that, when we see Jesus healing the sick, and feeding the hungry, and, above all, admitting the sinner and the outcast to his friendship, we can say: 'This is what God is like, and what he is like to me.'

That is why for me the Logos Doctrine of the first chapter of John's Gospel is the centre of my belief. I know well that distinguished theologians have said that the usefulness of that doctrine is outlived. Vincent Taylor in *The Person of Christ* quotes verdicts against it, and does not himself now find it useful. E. F. Scott says that, when all is said, the idea of the Logos 'was an artificial hypothesis, and was utterly inadequate to set forth the true significance of the revelation in Christ'. Leonard Hodgson says that its 'association with the doctrine of the Trinity has outlived its usefulness'. Vincent Taylor himself says that it did serve a providential purpose in the development of Christology, but 'it is not an idea with which Christian thought today can set out with confidence on the Christological quest'. I do not agree.

Stripped of the non-essentials, what does the Logos Doctrine mean? What does it mean to say that Jesus is the Logos? This word Logos has two meanings in Greek. It means *word* and it means *mind* or *reason*. There is no one English word which will translate both meanings. Take it in the sense of word. What is a word? A word is the expression of a thought. Therefore, Jesus is the expression of the thought of God. A word is the means of communication. Therefore, Jesus is God's means of communication with men. Take it in the sense of mind. To the Greek the Logos was that which put sense into the universe, that which made a cosmos out of a chaos, that which makes this a dependable world to live in, that which in spite of the change and flux of things still makes each seed give its own fruit, still makes each chemical combination result in the same thing, still keeps day and night and summer and winter in their appointed order, still keeps the planets in their courses, still makes man a thinking and a reasonable creature. And, quite simply, the Greek held that the Logos is nothing other than the mind of God in and through and above the universe and man. So, then, Jesus is the mind of God. The famous text: 'The word became flesh' (John 1:14) might well be translated: 'The mind of God became a person.'

So then, to put it at its simplest and its most essential, *I believe in a God who is like Jesus*. For me, the essential truth of Christianity is not so much that Jesus is like God, as it is that God is like Jesus. It is easy to see what a difference this belief makes. I have no longer to do with a God distant and terrifying; I have no longer to do with a God of inexorable justice; I have to do with a God who is intimate and understanding love.

Joachim Jeremias has seen the very essence of Christian belief in the new name that Jesus gave to God. Jesus called God *Abba* (Mark 14:36), and it is open to the Christian to do the same (Romans 8:15; Galations 4:6). Jeremias points out that *Abba* is far more than *father*; it was the word used by a little child to his father in the circle of the home. In secular Hebrew the translation of it would be Daddy. So Jeremias writes: 'Thus the first step in conversion and the new life is learning how to call God *Abba* with childlike confidence, safe under his protection, and conscious of his boundless love.' If we accept the principle that God is like Jesus, then the distant has become the near, the infinite has become the intimate, terror has turned to confidence and fear to love.

This is the God in whom I believe, but, having made this affirmation, I cannot leave it at that. If I believe in a God like that, how can I explain the sorrow and the suffering of the world? This is one of the oldest problems in the world, and for many one of the most acute. It is extraordinary how often this problem insists on emerging in the symposium *The God I want,* edited by James Mitchell. James Mitchell himself writes: 'No God is worth preserving unless he is of some practical use in curing the ills which plague humanity – all the disease and pain and starvation, the little children born crippled or spastic or mentally defective: a creator god would be answerable to us for these things at the day of judgment – if he dared to turn up.' William Miller in the same symposium insists that, even if in some future life, these wrongs are righted, the position is no better. 'It is no good tucking up a child in bed and giving it sweets after bullying it all day. The only acceptable God would be one who, having made a mistake in His creation, admitted His mistake and righted it.' 'The crimes of any divine act of creation are many and self-evident. ... To what divine purpose and in what loving brain was the scorpion forged? What holy chastening is intended when babies are being born deformed in mind or body? Is it God's will that two-thirds of the world's population are undernourished? ... Any hospital will show a gallery of pain which is almost unbearable to the viewers; a trip to the slum side of a town (excellently, these are decreasing in Britain and the United States) unmasks the unnecessary plight in which so many people in all times and places have passed their existence on earth ... If there is a God, he is responsible.'

No one is going to dismiss this problem with a wave of the hand, and no one is going to underestimate its agony. But even in these statements of it there is a clue to its solution, not a new solution, but the only solution which has reason in it. When we read these statements, we are bound to ask, Is it reasonable to blame God for the consequences of a drug which was not properly tested before it was used? Is it reasonable to blame God for the fact that two thirds of the world's population are undernourished when the remaining one third could mend the situation, if it would try? Is it reasonable to blame God for the mental condition of a child, if the child's parents either defied or took a risk with the laws of eugenics? Can we really say that in a hospital there is no one there because the laws of health have been broken, or because they have suffered from human cruelty and viciousness?

The old solution is still valid. If the relation between man and God is a relationship which is personal and which is grounded in love, then it cannot be other than voluntary, for love must ever be a free movement of heart to heart. However it may be explained, man has to have free will. As Suzanne de Dietrich said: 'Man is the only creature in the universe who can say "Yes" or "No" to God.' If man refuses to obey, then inevitably the consequences follow. Seneca said of God *amat fortiter*: he loves courageously, bravely, gallantly. His love is not a love which protects from the consequences; that would be to spoil, not to love, a child. If it be claimed that the innocent are involved in suffering, that is because in this world there is no such thing as an isolated individual. What happens to one, happens to all. No generation starts with a clean sheet. All good is transmitted and all evil is transmitted from one generation to another, and the one cannot be transmitted without the other.

The general truth still stands. Without free-will there can be no love; with free-will there is the possibility and even the certainty of disobedience; and with disobedience there come consequences; but the fault is with man. And there remains this to be said. Christianity does not claim to explain the problem of evil; but it does claim to give, and it gives, that which enables man to bear the unbearable and to do the undoable and even to turn the agony into a new discovery of God.

I believe in God, and I believe in a God who is like Jesus. I know that this is the affirmation of faith more than it is of reason; and I also know that in the last analysis all that one can say to anyone about an affirmation like this is: 'Act on it – and see what happens.' I began by speaking of the temperament which is inclined towards belief and the temperament which is not, and I end with a quotation which sums the thing up: 'To those who believe, no explanation is necessary. To those who disbelieve, no explanation is possible.' The Christian conviction of belief and the Christian adventure of faith can never be separated.

ANTHONY BLOOM,

Metropolitan of Sourozh, was born in Lausanne, June 19, 1914. His childhood was spent in Russia and Persia, his father being a member of the Russian Imperial Diplomatic Corps. His mother was the sister of Alexander Scriabin the composer. The family had to leave Persia during the Revolution and came to Paris where Archbishop Anthony was educated, graduating in Physics, Chemistry, and Biology, and taking his doctorate in Medicine, at the University of Paris. During World War II he served as an officer in the French Army until the fall of France, and then worked as a surgeon in one of the Paris hospitals and also took part in the Resistance. In 1943 he professed monastic vows while practising as a physician in Paris. In 1948 he was ordained to the priesthood and in 1949 came to England as Orthodox Chaplain to the Fellowship of St Alban and St Sergius, and in 1950 was appointed Vicar of the Russian Patriarchal Parish in London. In 1958 he was consecrated Bishop, and Archbishop in 1962, in charge of the Russian Church in Great Britain and Ireland. In 1963 he was also appointed Exarch to the Patriarch of Moscow in Western Europe, and in 1966 raised to the rank of Metropolitan. He takes an active part in inter-Church and ecumenical work, and was a member of the Russian Church delegation to the World Council of Churches in New Delhi in 1961 and in Geneva in 1966.

Publications: Somatopsychic Techniques (*translated into English and published in* 1957); Living Prayer, 1966.

ANTHONY BLOOM

I met Christ as a Person at a moment when I needed him in order to live, and at a moment when I was not in search of him. I was found; I did not find him. I was a teenager then. Life had been difficult in the early years and now it had of a sudden become easier. All the years when life had been hard I had found it natural, if not easy, to fight; but when life became easy and happy I was faced quite unexpectedly with a problem: I could not accept aimless happiness. Hardships and suffering had to be overcome, there was something beyond them. Happiness seemed to be stale if it had no further meaning. As it often happens when you are young and when you act with passion, bent to possess either everything or nothing, I decided that I would give myself a year to see whether life had a meaning, and if I discovered it had none I would not live beyond the year.

Months passed and no meaning appeared on the horizon. One day, it was during Lent, and I was then a member of one of the Russian youth organizations in Paris, one of our leaders came up to me and said, 'We have invited a priest to talk to you, come.' I answered with violent indignation that I would not. I had no use for Church. I did not believe in God. I did not want to waste any of my time. Then my leader explained to me that everyone who belonged to my group had reacted in exactly the same way, and if no one came we would all be put to shame because the priest had come and we would be disgraced if no one attended his talk. My leader was a wise man. He did not try to convince me that I should listen attentively to his words so that I might perhaps find truth in them: 'Don't listen,' he said. 'I don't care, but sit and be a physical presence.' That much loyalty I was prepared to give to my youth organization and that much indifference I was prepared to offer to God and to his minister. So I sat through the lecture, but it was with increasing indignation and distaste. The man who spoke to us, as I discovered later, was a great man, but I was then not capable of perceiving his greatness. I saw only a vision of Christ and of Christianity that was profoundly repulsive to me. When the lecture was over I hurried home in order to check the truth of what he had been saying. I asked my mother whether she had a book of the Gospel, because I wanted to know whether the Gospel would support the monstrous impression I had derived from this talk. I expected nothing good from my reading, so I counted the chapters of the four Gospels to be sure that I read the shortest, not to waste time unnecessarily. And thus it was the Gospel according to St Mark which I began to read.

I do not know how to tell you of what happened. I will put it quite simply and those of you who have gone through a similar experience will know what came to pass. While I was reading the beginning of St Mark's gospel, before I reached the third chapter, I became aware of a presence. I saw nothing. I heard nothing. It was no hallucination. It was a simple certainty that the Lord was standing there and that I was in the presence of him whose life I had begun to read with such revulsion and such ill-will.

This was my basic and essential meeting with the Lord. From then I knew that Christ did exist. I knew that he was *thou*, in other words that he was the Risen Christ. I met with the core of the Christian message, that message which St Paul formulated so sharply and clearly when he said, 'If Christ is not risen we are the most miserable of all men.' Christ *was* the Risen Christ for me, because if the One Who had died nearly 2000 years before was there alive, he was the *Risen* Christ. I discovered then something absolutely essential to the Christian message – that the Resurrection is the only event of the Gospel which belongs to history not only past but also present. Christ rose again, twenty centuries ago, but he *is* the Risen Christ as long as history continues. Only in the light of the Resurrection did everything else make sense to me. Because Christ was alive and I had been in his presence I could say with certainty that what the Gospel said about the Crucifixion of the prophet of Galilee was true, and the centurion was right when he said, 'Truly he is the Son of God'. It was in the light of the Resurrection that I could read with certainty the story of the Gospel, knowing that everything was true in it because the impossible event of the Ressurection was to me more certain than any event of history. History I had to believe, the Resurrection I knew for a fact. I did not discover, as you see, the Gospel beginning with its first message of the Annunciation, and it did not unfold for me as a story which one can believe or disbelieve. It began as an event that left all problems of disbelief because it was direct and personal experience.

Then I went on reading the Gospel and I discovered a certain number of things which I believe to be essential to the Christian faith, to the attitude of the Christian to the world and to God. The first thing that struck me is that God, as revealed to us in Christ, is everyone's God. He is not the God of a nation, or a confession, or of a denomination, or a more or less peculiar group, he is everyone's creator, Lord and Saviour. In him I discovered that the whole world had cohesion; that mankind was one; that differences and divergencies were not final and decisive, because we were loved of God; all of us equally, although we were called to serve him in a variety of ways, with a variety of gifts, and with a very different depth and width of knowledge. But the greater the knowledge, the greater the closeness, the greater the responsibility in a world that God loved so much that he gave his only begotten Son, for him to die that the world may live.

The second thing I discovered was that God not only does not want us to be subservient to him, but that he stands as none other for the dignity of man. He refuses to accept us as slaves; he does not permit us to forsake our dignity of sons and of children. Remember the parable of the Prodigal Son. In his humiliation the Prodigal Son is prepared to recognize that he is not worthy to be called any more a son, but in his longing to be accepted again into the forsaken household of the father he is prepared to be admitted into it as a servant. Yet when he comes to making his confession the father allows him to say, only 'I am not worthy to be called thy son,' but he interrupts him *then* because his son can be an unworthy son, but cannot be a worthy servant. Sonship is a gift that cannot be lost, although it can be profaned. This vision of a God who has respect for human dignity, who stands for it, who will not accept any debased relationship with man, filled me with admiration and with respect and with incipient love for him. And as a corollary – the acceptance by

God of utter humiliation and abasement. All the gods of the Ancient World were great: they were the sum total of all that was valued and admired – justice, wisdom, goodness, power. Only God revealed in Christ defeats human imagination, could not be invented by man: a God made in the image of the servant, vulnerable, despised, humiliated, rejected, contemptible, defeated, killed, ruled out, unredeemed in the eyes of men. A God no one would wish to invent or to have – a God one can discover when he reveals himself. A God one accepts with awe and with fear – because he calls us to be like him, upturning all values and giving new meaning to all things.

Then I discovered that *the world* was dear to God. That he had not only made the world to remain afterwards its Creator and become later its Judge. He had created the world in an act of love, and he had never become alient and indifferent to this world he had thus created. The Incarnation unfolded itself (and I am now speaking no longer of this first primeval experience of mine, but of something that has developed in the course of years), the Incarnation unfolded itself in a variety of meanings of depth. But not only of meanings, for the basic experience of *reality* remained always untouched.

When we read the Old Testament we may at moments think of the world once created by God moving and developing before the face of its Creator, and called one day to be judged. This vision is so poor and so inadequate to what the Old Testament teaches us. The fact that God called us, all the world visible and invisible, the fact that God called all things and beings out of nought, out of radical non-existence, into existence is already a relationship. We are related to God by this act of creation and in this act of creation. When we think that whatever and whoever he called into existence is called to be a companion of God for all eternity, we can see the depth of the divine love and the extent of the divine risk. Because we are free to accept the love of God and to reject it we can frustrate this love or fulfil this love. But God's love remains immutable and he remains faithful for ever. He creates each of us in hope and in faith, and at moments when our faith vacillates and our hope sways and wavers we can rest in the divine faith and in the divine hope. When we think that the cost of our faithlessness and our waverings is paid by God in the life and death of the Incarnate Word then we can rest assured in his love.

There is a relatedness and a deep relationship between us and God in the very act of creation, and in the very gift of freedom. Freedom is an absolute condition of love, because love is the gift of one's self in perfect freedom, and has no meaning apart from freedom. But there is more to it – the English word 'freedom' is rooted in the Old English word that means 'beloved'; 'my free' meant 'my beloved'. The word Liberty which signifies freedom in other languages defines the status of the child born free in a freeman's household. The Russian word for freedom indicates that we are called to be our own selves, not to imitate, not to ape, not to resemble, but to be ourselves in the image of the One who is perfect freedom and perfect love – truly himself. In all this the relatedness there exists between us and God is revealed particularly in this final act of *solidarity* which we call the Incarnation. Not only did God remain concerned with us throughout history, but he became one of us through history, and this not for a moment, but forever; not escaping the heaviness, the limitations and the pain of our human destiny, but in order to carry on his human shoulders the consequences of his divine act of creation and of our human rebellion, our rejection of him, lovelessness, godlessness itself. The Incarnation of the Word of God, the becoming man, meant for him that he entered into the realm of time and of death and of limitation and of all the consequences of human godlessness. This solidarity was not for a moment, it was definitive. He became a man, in human history, and he remains a man for ever because 'He sitteth on the right hand of the Father' as a man with hands and feet pierced by the nails, and with his side pierced by the spear. Throughout history and throughout eternity we can see this vision of divine solidarity with us.

This solidarity goes infinitely further than we often imagine. It is not simply that he was tired and hungry and thirsty, that he had to face ill-will and unfriendliness and eventually hatred. He had to face something more basic to our mortal condition and more essential than this. He had to face the coming of death and the actual dying. This is more than we can imagine, because in the natural course of events Christ *could not* die! A human body and a human soul united indissolubly and for ever with the God-head in the mystery and the miracle of the Incarnation was beyond dying. Death was not only like ours – a result of our lack of life – it was the result of an act of divine will which inflicted death on One who was, not only in his Divinity but even in his humanity, alive with life eternal, because life is defined by oneness or union with God. We see him in the garden on the Mount of Olives face to face with death coming upon him, abandoned by human friendship; by those who were his disciples and were no longer solid with his destiny at that moment. He accepted death, which meant already the loss of what was his own being in life. Again upon the Cross the decisive, the most tragic words of history: 'My God, my God, why hast Thou forsaken Me?' Why? Because death is possible *only* through separation from the source of life, from the Godhead, and for him to die meant that he went through the experience of total, radical, real deprivation of God; of godlessness not only as a world-outlook, not only as an absence of the sense of God, but as a positive loss of the Father. There is not one man on earth who can claim to have known godlessness as Christ knew the absence of God at that moment, without which absence he could not die. This is the extent of the divine solidarity with us. This also is the measure of the divine love and consideration God has for the friend he has created to be his companion of all eternity. People are often prepared to believe in the death of the Cross but not in the Resurrection. How strange! To believe that life can die, and not to be able to believe that life can *live*. How strange also that we are so poor in the experience of things of our own faith that the only event of history which belongs to our own day is so obscure, and we do not know the Risen Christ while we imagine we are capable of knowing the Christ of the flesh; that Christ of whom Paul said, that we do not know him any more while we now know the Christ of the Spirit, revealed and known to us by the Spirit of God.

But in Christ we do not discover only this Divine solidarity and incipiently, as I have tried to show, the value which God attaches to us. We discover also what man is, because he is not only Very God he is also Very Man. Our vocation is to be what he is. This is the meaning of our belief in the Church as the Body of Christ.

We are called to be live, real members of a real enlived body, the head of which is the Lord Jesus – one real body, what St Ignatius of Antioch in the first century called the 'Total Christ', Head and Body together. We are called to such intimate community of life with him that what he *is* we also are to become, in the words of one of the greatest writers of the fourth century, Athanasius of Alexandria, who says, 'God has become man in order that we should become gods'. Before we become gods we must become men in the image of the One who became what we are. The extent to which we are called to be identified with him who chose to be identified with us is greater than we think. It is because we have a very mean vision of our calling that we are not aiming at the full stature of Christ. Irenaeus of Lyons taught in the second century that, if it is true that we are the Body of Christ, that in him we are one, that our life is hid with Christ in God, then the final vocation of men is, together with Christ because of our oneness with him, to become the only-begotten son of God, an extension in time and in space and in eternity of this incredible, unfathomable relatedness and relationship with the Father.

In that sense we can say soberly, yet with what exultation, that Christ is the very centre of history as he is the beginning of all things ('by the Word were all things created') and the end of all things, because in him, by the power of the Holy Spirit, we shall in our total humanity have reached to the fullness of our human vocation and God shall be all in all. When we think of the life of Christ and of the death of Christ it is with anguish that we think of the extraordinary insensitiveness and indifference with which we partake in what we see in him. The act of perfect intercession, the act by which he took a step that brought him to the core of the human tragedy; the act by which he became that man of whom the Book of Job speaks in the ninth chapter, who could take his stand between God and one who was judged by God, in order to bring both together. The One who is an equal of both and therefore can bring them together in his own self, but also at his own cost, because every act of intercession is an act of sacrifice.

I would like to illustrate this vision of a sacrifice and its consequences for us by something taken from the late history of the

Russian Church. In the years of the Civil War when the opposing armies were contending for power, conquering and losing ground in the course of three years, a small town fell into the hands of the Red army which had been held by the remnants of the Imperial troops. A woman found herself there with her two small children, four and five years of age, in danger of death because her husband belonged to the opposite camp. She hid in an abandoned house hoping that the time would come when she would be able to escape. One evening a young woman of her own age, in the early twenties, knocked at the door and asked her whether she was so-and-so. When the mother said she was, the young woman warned her that she had been discovered and would be fetched that very night in order to be shot. The young woman added, 'You must escape at once.' The mother looked at the children and said, 'How could I?' The young neighbour, who thus far had been nothing but a physical neighbour, became at that moment the neighbour of the Gospel. She said, 'You can, because I will stay behind and call myself by your name when they come to fetch you.' 'But you will be shot,' said the mother. 'Yes, but I have no children.' And she stayed behind.

We can imagine what happened then. We can see the night coming, wrapping in darkness, in gloom, in cold and damp, this cottage. We can see there a woman who was waiting for her death to come and we can remember the Garden of Gethsemane. We can imagine this woman asking that this cup should pass her by and being met like Christ by divine silence. We can imagine her turning in intention towards those who might have supported her, but who were out of reach. The disciples of Christ slept; and she could turn to no one without betraying. We can imagine that more than once she prayed that at least her sacrifice should not be in vain, and here we can see the image of another man who stood before death and hesitated. The greatest of those born to a woman, John the Baptist, who as death was coming to him, sent two of his disciples to Christ to ask him, 'Is it really you, or should we expect another one?' If it is really you then all the sacrifices of my youth, all the years in the wilderness; all the hatred I was surrounded by; the coming of death; my diminishing in order that you might grow, is a blessedness; but if it is not you then I have lost my life,

I have lived and I shall die in vain. Here again the prophet received the reply of the prophet, but no word of consolation.

This young woman probably asked herself more than once what would happen to the mother and the children when she was dead, and there was no reply except the word of Christ, 'No one has greater love than he who lays down his life for his friend.' Probably she thought more than once that in one minute she could be secure! It was enough to open the door and the moment she was in the street she no longer was that woman, she became herself again. It was enough to deny her false, her shared identity. We can see again one of the strongest men in history, Peter the apostle, challenged by a woman in the coldness of night and in his desperate loneliness denying in order to save his life. She died, shot. The mother and the children escaped, and here we see one more thing which will be the last I wish to mention.

St Paul tells us, 'It is no longer I who live, it is Christ who lives in me.' We often wonder at the meaning of these words. How can Christ live in one? We can have an inkling of this meaning from the life of this mother and her children. They remained alive because another died. They have remained aware throughout their lives that they lived on borrowed life. Their life was cut off the earth by the hatred of men and it was given back by the love of this woman. If they were alive it was because she had lived; her life was theirs. They had to live and fulfil her life. They had to live as she had taught them. Is not this something which we can learn also? Is not this what we must learn from the act of perfect solidarity which we find in the Incarnation, from the insuperable courage and love of God, from the Garden of Gethsemane and the death upon the Cross? Solidarity not only between ourselves, but with every man, because God is solid with the godless as with the saint. The victory of life is in us not only because we receive the miraculous gift of life from God, but because if we live as he taught us he will be alive in us, and we shall be alive in him, now and for all eternity.

COLIN BROWN

was born in Bradford. He read German at the Universities of Liverpool and Erlangen. After national service with the Intelligence Corps in the Canal Zone he trained for the Anglican ministry at Tyndale Hall, Bristol. He was ordained in 1958. During his curacy he did research at the University of Nottingham on Karl Barth. In 1961 he joined the staff of Tyndale Hall, where he is now Vice-Principal. He is married and has two girls and a boy. Publications include contributions to various symposia and Karl Barth and the Christian Message *(Tyndale Press, 1967). Hobbies: family, painting (house and water colours) and listening to music. Special interests: historical theology and the study of the gospels.*

COLIN BROWN

Path to Faith

I suppose that I have always had some sort of belief in God, though I have not always professed the Christian faith. As a rather small schoolboy I used to pray desperately about examinations, only to dispense with the Almighty's services once the immediate hurdle was safely cleared. Later on I found it convenient to don the armour of sixth-form bravado and enter the fray of theological debate under the banner of an amused but tolerant scepticism. And for a while I found many of my agnostic arguments convincing. At least they were good at exposing cant in others (though not in myself) and sweeping into oblivion all forms of organized religion. Even so, I kept having nagging doubts about my doubts.

Modern history happened to be among the subjects I was reading. I could not help being impressed by men like Luther and John Wesley. It was not just that they had taken out insurance policies for eternity and had done something useful with their lives into the bargain. There seemed to be something in it after all.

It was at university that I finally came to believe that man cannot live by scepticism alone. Nor was it possible to live on the meagre diet of materialism (whether Marxist, capitalist, or that of the student whose only thoughts are to pass his examinations as a passport to a safe, faceless existence in suburbia). Luther and the Reformers kept coming back at me. Goethe's *Faust* and Pascal's *Pensées* kept raising awkward questions about the meaning of existence.

But for all that, my mind was torn. I could see that the New Testament called men to a way of life that was higher than anything anyone else had devised either before or since. But there were problems. Could I be sure that God exists? Could I be sure that the figure of Jesus was not the product of pious imagination? Moreover, there were sides to the Church which were not altogether enthralling.

I always had a sneaking suspicion that men in dog collars were not quite honest or at best well-meaning but muddle-headed. Even now it dies hard. If only one could have the simplicity of the Christ of the Gospels without the humbug of the Church! In my innocence I little realized how deep-seated that humbug could be. But I had also yet to realize the meaning of Christian fellowship and the self-effacing goodness of Christian people. That ridiculous clerical garb was still more suggestive of a character in a Whitehall Theatre farce than of a man of God. The possibility that it might be otherwise was a revelation that still lay in the future for me.

Church services did not always help. I could stomach sermons and prayers. The embarrassment of not being able to find my way about the Prayer Book was soon overcome by simple practice. But it was the hymns that were the real bugbear. Apart from the physical difficulty of singing them, many of them told of a world that was so different from mine. I just did not want to dwell for ever in marble halls filled with golden light. The power of hymns is so persuasive that when many of us become Christians, we learn to speak, think and pray in a kind of Victoriana. But it is as remote from real life as those prints of highland stags which used to decorate the walls of seedy, pre-war, seaside boarding-houses.

Looking back on those restless, undergraduate days of wandering, certain landmarks stand out. I must owe a good deal to C. S. Lewis, although I never met him in person. The salty common sense of *The Screwtape Letters*, coupled with Lewis's gift for asking the right questions, helped a lot towards seeing the trees as well as the wood. Discussion with other students also played a big part. But the first milestone was reached – I might almost say tripped over – when I accidentally strayed into a university mission where I was amazed to hear a Christian speaker argue cogently for the Christian faith. So far, belief in God had been one thing and the faith of the Christian Church something quite different. Once I was persuaded in the weeks that followed that Christianity could be honestly and intelligently defended, the rest was almost downhill.

But in the end, the real difficulty was not intellectual at all. It seemed to me then – as it still does now – that a half-hearted Christian is a contradiction in terms. Whether or not a man succeeds in the Christian life is another matter. Jesus came not for the righteous but for sinners. But it was for penitent sinners – sinners who wanted to be different. And this was the real rub. The only thing that the Christ of the gospels has to offer is a package deal. If you want God, then you have to put up with his ways. If you want to walk with God, the first step is to put yourself into his hands without reserve and go on from there. This was the snag. We all want to have our cake and eat it. Supposing that God wanted me to become one of those dreadful parsons or (what was worse) a missionary? I could see it coming, and the prospects looked bleak. But it was no good. I fought it off as long as I could. I had no peace of mind until I gave up the unequal struggle.

On the day that I went up to university my father had given me a Bible just in case I might need it. The gift was accepted, though with some incredulity as to what earthly or heavenly contingency might induce me to resort to its use. Even after I had come to a Christian faith my reading of it was rather desultory. But as the weeks and months went by, its pages put life in a new perspective. It was as if a new dimension had been added to life.

My attendances at public worship were at first equally sparse. In the early days they were dogged by fear: fear of being pounced upon once I was inside the church doors and fear of what others might think once it got around that I was going to church. I tried different denominations. In the end I became an Anglican, and was confirmed in my final year at university. From time to time I almost have to pinch myself to make sure that I am not just dreaming all this. It is not that I am really something else underneath, wistfully hankering after non-conformity or Rome. I have never for one moment regretted becoming an Anglican. But in my teens Anglicanism was synonymous with dressing up and stuffy, ecclesiastical bureaucracy. What attracted me to the Church of England – and still does – were its Thirty-Nine Articles, its Prayer Book and the fellowship of those of its number who are trying to live out the Christian life. For all its faults (which were duly increased when its ranks were swollen at my confirmation), it still preserves a good deal of vital, New Testament Christianity.

If you want to pin me down and ask what label best fits me (and I don't see why not), my reply is that I am an Anglican in the reformed, evangelical tradition. For of all the traditions it is this one that seems to come closest to New Testament faith and practice. But like the first Anglican Reformers, I have no wish to cut loose from other members of the Church down the ages. No one group has a monopoly of truth. I firmly believe in dialogue both with other Christians and with non-Christians, but not in the sham sort which pretends that differences do not exist or do not matter. Progress is made (or so it seems to me) when we take seriously the great thinkers of other traditions, like Aquinas, Luther and Calvin, and look fairly and squarely at the really big problems.

If you were to ask who I thought was the most significant theologian of modern times I would say Karl Barth without any hesitation. Like Barth himself, I am not a Barthian. I think that at certain crucial points Barth takes the wrong turning. But there is no thinker today from whom more can be learnt, whether it be from his insights or from his mistakes. He sees the big issues in depth. He has never been one to be fobbed off with facile answers or carried away by theological fashion. He looks at questions in the light of the answers given by the great thinkers of the past and present. Above all, he brings to them a profound and penetrating understanding of the Bible.

To say that I believe in God is not the same as saying that I know all the answers. It seems to me that every article of the Christian faith begins and ends in mystery. I shall return to this in a few moments. But in the meantime it seems to me that belief in God is neither more easy nor more difficult than it was in bygone generations. Each one of us has to make his own spiritual pilgrimage. I am, therefore, sceptical of basing belief merely on the authority of the Church, as if sheer antiquity could serve as a guarantee of truth. But I am equally sceptical of TV theologians who talk as if their doubts and dilemmas had suddenly been thrust upon them overnight, and by some kind of verbal juggling turn doubt into faith. There is very little in the present theological situation that had not been well aired a hundred years ago. The idea that the gospels were full of myth was energetically canvassed by D. F. Strauss in the 1830s. The news that God was dead was brought to the world by Nietzsche in the palmy days of Queen Victoria. And the thought of the world coming of age (and therefore not recognizing any authority outside man himself) was expounded by Kant in 1784.

But enough of this. It is high time I put my own cards on the table and say why I believe in God.

Belief in God

There was a time in my life when my heart ached for 'objective proof'. The Christian faith was all very well, but it seemed so subjective. Some people might well content themselves with saying that to travel hopefully was better than to arrive. But not me. If we are not going to get anywhere with religion, I just don't want to go. If religion is just a matter of enlarging and deepening my self-understanding, I can get that sort of thing better from novels, the theatre and TV. And without the bother of going to church and the charade of saying prayers to a God who is not really there.

What I wanted was some 'objective proof' *outside* the Christian faith itself that God was there all the time and that the basic tenets of the Christian faith were true after all. In other words, I was looking for a valid natural theology. But I am not sure now that this is the right way to approach religion.

From Thomas Aquinas in the Middle Ages onwards philosophers have tried to find rational proofs of the existence of God which could then serve as a foundation for faith (whether Christian or otherwise). The list of illustrious names of those who have embarked upon this quest include those of Descartes, Berkeley, Spinoza and Leibniz. Among the proofs adduced are the so-called cosmological and teleological arguments. The former argues back to a first cause of everything; the latter to a great designer of the universe. Thus we might say, nothing that we know causes (or, for that matter designs) itself. If we press back far enough we must assume a first cause or designer for everything, alias God.

But this type of argument is apt to have something of the qualities of a mirage. At best it gives us a hypothetical cause which appears to have substance by reason of the fact that we pin a name to it. But in reality it is hidden from the grasp of the human mind behind the teeming millions of secondary causes. And for the unwary pursuer of such a notion there are all kinds of intellectual booby-traps concealed along the way. If we can say that everything must have a cause outside itself, we are caught on the inevitable rebound by the question: Who caused God? Even if we try to side-step this one by saying that there must have been a first cause of some sort, or the whole process would never have started, we are soon enmeshed in a web of philosophical puzzles. How do we show that there is only one God? Logically we are not entitled to attribute to any cause qualities other than those required to produce the effect in question. How then do we prove logically that there is only one ultimate cause of the universe? How do we demonstrate that the first cause is the same as the great designer? And how do we show that these notions that we accept by reason (granting for the moment that the arguments are valid) are one and the same as the triune God that Christians believe in by faith?

In short, attempts to prove the truth of Christian faith by such 'objective' arguments seem to me to be rather dubious. On the other hand, in the face of the myriads of complex mechanisms in nature I find it impossible to accept that it is all the result of pure chance.

In real life, however, very few people seem to be moved by hypothetical questions. God may play little more than a walking-on part in our lives. But very few of us are convinced, militant atheists. The reason for this seems to be the very simple one that most of us are aware of God in the depths of our beings. It may be difficult to formulate and even harder to communicate. (It would be surprising if it were otherwise, for God is not an object of time and space.) It might mean more for some of us, if we did as Paul Tillich has suggested, and scrap the word *God* for the time being. At least it may help to remove some of the cobwebs until we are ready to understand what it stands for. No doubt our awareness of God comes and goes. Often it is dim. But when we look into the depths of our consciousness we are aware of a being who stands over against us whom we just cannot explain away. We are aware of him in a way that is different from our awareness of furniture, cars, motorways and even people. I use the word 'him' advisedly. For this being who at times seems utterly remote is not in the last analysis alien. He does not always answer in the ways we expect, but he hears the cries of those who call.

My approach to belief in God is, therefore, not the two-storey one of the older natural theology which tries to build the ground floor by reason and the top floor by faith. The foundations which at first sight might seem impressive do not, on closer inspection, seem capable of bearing the weight of faith. There is always the difficulty of fastening faith to reason in this way and the attendant danger of the top floor being blown off by a sudden gust of scepticism.

To my mind, the right approach is summed up in the words of Anselm, one of the greatest of all archbishops of Canterbury: *Credo ut intelligam* ('I believe so that I may understand').[1] It is not a case of proving first and then believing. Natural theology puts the cart before the horse. It is only as we encounter God that we are in a position to explore and understand our relationship with him. Both faith and reason play their part. Without faith – without commitment, prayer and trust – there can be no intimate encounter. Without reason there can be neither apprehension nor understanding. To me belief is reasonable not in the sense that it can be proved beforehand. It is reasonable because it is warranted by experience.

Christian Belief

It has been said that the difference between other religions and Christianity is that Christians know God as their Father. I think that this is true. Christianity is a religion to live and die by, or it is nothing at all. This was the testimony of the Church down the ages from the early martyrs to the Reformers, the Puritans and their successors. We encounter it today in writings as diverse as Bonhoeffer's *Letters and Papers from Prison* and the book which provided the story for *The Sound of Music*, *The Trapp Family Singers*. It is the message of every page of the New Testament. It finds expression in the heights and depths of human experience in the Psalms of Israel.

At the heart of Christian belief stands the covenant relationship by which God has pledged himself to his people with the

[1] *Proslogion*, i.

promise: I will be your God and you shall be my people.[1] In the religion of Israel this relationship found symbolic expression in the gift of the Promised Land and all that went with it. At the Last Supper Jesus declared that his death was inaugurating a new covenant.[2] Unlike the old one which was tied to the institutions of Israel, the new covenant is one which all men are invited to enter.

The God of Christian belief is not the remote God of philosophical contemplation. He steps into history, and deals with men personally. He spoke to Israel by the prophets, and still speaks to men today through their witness and that of the New Testament writers. By this I do not simply mean that these writers had certain religious experiences which they later interpreted and put down on paper in their own words (rather like schoolboy essays written on the first day of the new term describing what they had done in the holidays). Of course, what they wrote was the distillation of their own experiences. But often they claim that what they wrote was written under the constraint of God himself, so that they were in a sense the mouthpieces of God.

The biblical writings could well be described as sacramental. In the Lord's Supper the bread and wine remain bread and wine and yet become vehicles of divine encounter. So scripture remains the word of man, bearing all the marks of human authorship, reflecting particular circumstances and human reactions, and yet at the same time it is the medium of divine-human encounter.

How does one know all this? The question is a fair one. To my mind, the answer is twofold. On the one hand, we may point to the claims that the biblical writers make for their utterances, as, for example, when they said, 'Thus saith the Lord . . .' Throughout his life Jesus himself was conscious of a constraint not to set aside this word, but to live by it and fulfil it. His own teaching was of the same order. When he himself taught, he taught as one who had divine authority and not like one of the scribes. On the other hand, we may point to the testimony of Christians down the ages that these writings have brought light and meaning to them in their perplexities, their loneliness, their trials, their

---

[1] Leviticus 26:12; cf. Genesis 12, 15, 17; Exodus 24; Jeremiah 31: 31ff; 2 Corinthians 6:16, etc.

[2] Matthew 26:28; Mark 14:24; 1 Corinthians 11:25.

joyful days and their humdrum days; that through these writings they have heard the voice of God. But, it may be asked, how do they know? In the last analysis the answer seems to me to be rather like learning to recognize colours. We know that this thing is yellow and that thing is red, when we see them. The colours cannot be reduced to terms other than their own. We know them by a kind of intuition. So it is with the Christian experience of God. In and through the welter of human feelings we become aware of someone who is *other* and who commands our obedience.

Let me hasten to add that this is not a kind of knock-down argument designed to win the assent of all and sundry without further ado. The biblical writers themselves have much to say on the difficulties and conditions of knowing God. It is never a purely intellectual affair. In the Sermon on the Mount Jesus said that the gate is narrow and the way hard that leads to life.[1] Seeking is a prior condition to finding.[2] The way is found only by walking with Jesus himself.[3]

For the Christian, belief in God is inseparable from belief in Christ. The New Testament presents Jesus as the one who truly reveals the Father and bridges the gulf between God and man. It is through him that our alienation is overcome. He is the culmination of all that has gone before. It is through him that we know God as our Father. This has always been the scandal of Christian faith. But in the nineteenth century the veracity of the New Testament picture of Jesus came under heavy fire, and in recent years the attack has been renewed not so much by outsiders as by a certain type of theologian inside the Church. Can we accept the Gospels today as trustworthy accounts of Jesus? There are scholars like Rudolf Bultmann who argue that what they give is not a picture of Jesus as he was, but the product of the creative imagination of the early Church. The resurrection of Jesus was not a historical event but the mythical expression of the Easter faith of the first Christians.

If Bultmann is right, I could not honestly remain a Christian. I might still have religious experiences, but the Christian expla-

[1] Matthew 7:14.
[2] Matthew 7:7f.
[3] John 14:6; cf. 7:17; Luke 14; 26f, 33.

nation of them would no longer hold. For the Christian faith is essentially faith in what God in Christ has done in history. It is faith in God reconciling the world to himself through the death and resurrection of Jesus. If it did not happen, we have no gospel left. It seems to me that this is what St Paul had in mind when he pointed out to the Church at Corinth that, 'If Christ has not been raised, then our preaching is in vain and your faith is in vain'.[1]

But the more I study Bultmann (and it seems to me right that those who hold views like mine should frankly face the objections), the less convincing I find him. He seems to me to be singularly lacking in historical insight and method. The more I study the Gospels, the more I find myself in agreement with J. B. Phillips when he speaks of their 'ring of truth'.[2] Honest doubt can be satisfied only by honest and patient investigation. But it seems to me that such honest and patient investigation leads to very different results from those canvassed by some of our more radical theologians.

This is obviously not the place to attempt a historical appraisal of the New Testament. But in view of the cruciality of the question, I hope that the reader who has followed me so far will pardon a couple of cross references to books which seem to me to put things in perspective. The first is relatively recent and gives an overall reappraisal. It is Professor F. F. Bruce's *The New Testament Documents: Are They Reliable?* (1960). The second is over fifty years old and deals specifically with the historical question of the resurrection. It is James Orr's *The Resurrection of Jesus*. Obviously, it does not treat recent writers, but it is thoroughly aware of the problems involved and of the great debates of the nineteenth century which were no less acute than those of today.

The more I try to live out the Christian life and the more I study theology (both ancient and modern), the more I am driven to the Christ of the historic creeds of the Church. I cannot understand how Jesus can be both God and man, or how God can be Father, Son and Holy Spirit and still be the one God. These are what the older theologians called mysteries. They seem to in-

---

[1] 1 Corinthians 15:14.
[2] Cf. J. B. Phillips, *Ring of Truth: A Translator's Testimony*, 1967.

volve contradictions, and yet each part of the contradiction is warranted. If one aspect is pressed to the exclusion of the other, or if both are allowed to cancel each other out, the result is a distortion or a denial of the evidence. The early Church went through four hundred years of such teething troubles, and now it seems that we are going through them all over again. Some thought then that Jesus was an inspired man who walked closely with God. Others denied his humanity altogether. Still others sought a compromise which made him neither one nor the other but something in between. It is fashionable these days to snipe at the creeds. But at least they show themselves more aware of the issues involved than some of their critics. And they avoid short-cut solutions which in the end create more problems than they solve.

Physicists tell me that they encounter the same sort of problem in the natural sciences. It makes good sense to think of light in terms of both waves and particles. Neither view can be ruled out. But it is equally impossible to harmonize the two. Now all this might not fit in very well with preconceived, rationalistic ideas. But reality is often like that. Mysteries in the theological sense may be insoluble. But every genuine mystery is posited on good grounds. And although they are inexplicable in themselves, mysteries have the quality of throwing light on the darker areas of experience.

It seems to me that sooner or later every major Christian affirmation leads to a mystery. We do not understand the nature of God. We do not understand the ways in which he works in the physical world. We do not really understand why God allows evil. There are, of course, partial explanations for some things. We can see that, in giving man freedom, God was making a nobler creature than a mere automaton, even though this was at the risk of man's misuse of freedom. But this does not always explain why the innocent suffer. Mysteries enable us to see part of the way but not the whole way.

As creatures of time and space, we have to think in terms of objects of time and space. This is all right, of course, when we think about physical objects like cats, cars and rockets to the moon. But it raises difficulties when we try to think about God who is not an object that we can look at in time and space. In recent years linguistic philosophers have given a good deal of thought to the meaning and status of religious language. It seems to me that Thomas Aquinas in the Middle Ages was already on the right lines when he said that our language about God was *analogical*. When we call God our Father, we are not speaking the strict literal truth. God is not an enlarged human being who has brought children into the world by natural procreation. But there are genuine similarities between all that is best in human fatherhood and God. We know it to be so, because this image comes to us through the revelation that was given through the biblical writers and supremely through Jesus himself. We know it to be so, because we find that there is a real similarity between our human experiences of fatherhood and our religious experiences of God.

Again it would be desirable to develop this theme. But I can do no more than commend to the interested reader two writers who have thought constructively and suggestively on this subject: Ian T. Ramsey, *Religious Language* (1957) and E. L. Mascall, *Words and Images* (1957).

In my earlier days as a Christian, I cannot say that I got very worked up about sin. I had a dull, aching sense of need. What attracted me was the sense of purpose, fulfilment and service that I saw in the Gospels. I knew others who took sin seriously, and I began to get worried whether there was anything wrong with me, because I did not. I need not have bothered. Awareness of human failings came soon enough.

When we measure ourselves by the Gospel's standards, we cannot go far without realizing how hollow are all our pretensions in reality. In the last analysis the real problems of religion are not our fads and our intellectual puzzles but our alienation from each other and from God. But by his death and resurrection Christ has overcome the estrangement. Like the father in the Parable of the Prodigal Son, God waits for us to return. But the God I believe is one who does more than wait. He sends his Son to bring us home.

ELSIE CHAMBERLAIN

was educated at Channing School, studied Speech, Music and Art, taught Violin and elocution and worked as a dress designer before going to King's College, London to take a B.D. and enter the Congregational Ministry. She ministered in Liverpool, London, Richmond, Surrey, and as Chaplain in the R.A.F. (the only woman Chaplain in H.M. Forces). From 1950 to 1967 she was on the staff of the B.B.C. Religious Department, responsible for Lift Up Your Hearts *and* Silver Lining. *She was Chairman of the Congregational Union of England and Wales, 1956-7.*

Born in London the ecumenical daughter of a Congregational mother and an Anglican father, she is ecumenically married to the Rector of Greensted, Ongar, Essex.

ELSIE CHAMBERLAIN

To begin with, belief in God was an inheritance; though whether I mean by that, that it was in the flesh and blood and brain and bone of the baby that was me, or whether I learned it or caught it or was taught it, I can't say.

But it was there in our home. I remember my earliest prayer – to 'Thee', not 'you'. It wouldn't be approved of now. And Mother always read the Bible aloud at breakfast. At a school-friend's home I remember her father read the Bible – at length, it seemed, – *before* breakfast; and then we all knelt down with the smell of bacon and fried bread on the air. He was a dear man and enjoyed talking to God, but I don't remember the prayers; I wanted my breakfast. While she read the portion for the day, I can still see my Mother's breakfast balanced on her cup to keep warm while we got on with ours.

Sunday was the day! There must have been a lot of people to share their belief in God with the children of those days. There was Sunday School before Morning Service. I remember my older brothers dashing off after breakfast, though this had stopped before I was old enough to go; and there was afternoon Sunday School, all in separate classes, and a Children's Separate Service at six o'clock. It would have been hard not to believe in God with so many people ready to teach you about Him.

There were the Sunday Hats too! When I think of them there is no more spirit in me. I don't often wear a hat now.

But it was a great day – an accepted family day; and it was accepted that my father always went off in a different direction to sing in his Church of England choir. Some people said 'How funny!' ('peculiar' they meant). But not a bit of it! That was our family. And when one brother at the University stage was too busy to worship God, I was somehow aware of the prayerful concern for him.

Just at the stage when it would have been my turn to kick over the traces and revolt against church-going and express doubt rather than belief, all my initiative and energy and spare time were drawn by shortage of leaders into the down-town church that was 'ours'. The struggle at seventeen to teach boys of eleven to fourteen and the presents they brought me after being particularly demon-possessed! The wild and gigantic schemes to raise money in the 'thirties. No affluence, no 'plenty of other people to do it'. In face of all the difficulties I was quite sure it was God's work – and urgent.

I was twenty when the Rev. Robert Shepherd came to be our Minister. I suppose he was 'old-fashioned' in some ways. He started a 'Christian Endeavour', and that was the beginning of my study of theology – a very simple beginning, but he was a scholar and loved to evoke the questions of the young. And we evolved painlessly from a narrow fundamentalism into exciting new heights and depths; the Bible came alive, and he himself taught me Hebrew.

I think it was chiefly through him, and later through the Rev. Muriel Paulden (and it's humbling to wonder why I should have had two such teachers), that I became aware why and how theology is the Queen of Sciences. Again, I seem to have been born with a respect for superior knowledge and therefore a readiness to learn that lots of people do not have. So because I knew that every scientist has to accept some basis from which to work, I was able to accept a working hypothesis, a basis of belief in God; and as in any lesser science, so in theology one experiments from that basis.

The first essential to my belief is the basic goodness of life that depends on the goodness of the mind behind it all; and many have agreed that there must be a mind, and that everything from a baby to a dewdrop cannot be just fortuitous.

My teachers lived by the belief that this 'Mind' is personal. So this again I accepted at least as a basis for experiment.

One wonders at the immensity, the complexity of the mind behind the movement of mountains and the wobble in the warbler's song; one needs the sinful egotism of human nature to be able to dare claim a personal relationship with power so vast. So again I look for a reason for my unreasonable conceit.

I see the reason in a poor child of doubtful parentage – born inconveniently and unhygienically to a couple displaced by the red tape of a foreign bureaucracy and its imposition of a new tax. For most nations, respect for motherhood came centuries after that child's birth; there was no welfare state to put a woman-great-with-child in the front of a queue for lodgings; a stable was the best they could find.

But the baby was born, and by some gift of second sight (we won't argue about that for the moment) various odd and quite different characters recognized a super-natural element, some fulfilment of age-long hope and prophecy, in the child.

He grew up in the home of the carpenter of Nazareth. Here and there throughout his life different people felt or saw something unusual about him. Not often. Not enough to convince them beyond doubt that they were not just 'seeing things' or 'hearing voices'.

Came a day when the young carpenter (the old one seems to have died by then) stood up in the local synagogue and claimed that he was the fulfilment of Isaiah's prophecy about a Messiah. And those people who had known him from a child would have pushed him headfirst over the cliff – if he had not 'gone on his way'. They liked local boys to make good, but not too good.

Soon he had established his campaign by inviting twelve men to be his followers. They fell in for more than they had bargained for: excitement, surprises, shocks, and a perpetual uncertainty: who is this? by what authority? what wisdom is this that has been given him? Where does he get it from? How does he work such miracles? Is not this the carpenter? Sometimes they were afraid: the time three of them saw the man they had elected to follow shining with supernatural light, talking with two great men of the past: when, in critical times he 'set his face' to go to Jerusalem, straight into danger. But something, they found, wiped off on them. 'In his name' *they* could cast out devils and heal the sick, and he told them to be more excited that their names were written in heaven.

What did that mean? Were they allies of God? They found the hypothesis from which they worked was constantly changing as the impossible became possible and the improbable a fact of experience.

51

Was it true that 'no man ever spoke as this man speaks'? If so, who could he be?

There were indications of second sight, also of new insight that came to his friends through their experiences with him. Measure this and his way of life generally by any known standard of goodness, and what happens? He sticks out beyond the standards so far that he is his own standard.

So I come back to *my* working hypothesis and take it to be that he is the most perfect man who ever lived; and I must find out how my experience deals with this. Unlike the other good Jews of his day, can I excuse the legal blasphemy of his claim to be one with God? Or can I take my hypothesis a bit farther still and try working from the idea that he was God-in-a-human-form? I begin to see that no lesser explanation stands up to experiment or experience, and to know that all my experiments from this new hypothesis are increasing my experience of the truth that was in Jesus. And the uniqueness about his standard lies especially in his concern for *all* sorts and conditions of men and women. His teaching about God is of one who is so concerned with our life in all its detail that even the hairs of our heads have all been counted; that though sparrows are five for twopence, not one of them is overlooked by God; and, said Jesus, 'you are worth more than any number of sparrows'. He demonstrated and taught the infinite capacity of God to love all his creatures.

As far as I know this is the uniqueness that makes the Christian belief in God different from any other peoples' belief in a god. I remember a centenarian parson who summed up his accumulated philosophy of life in one phrase – 'Everyone is first with God'. That's it. And if you find it possible to believe God loves you, you daren't believe that anyone else is less loved than you. This is hard, but it is basic to the whole of the faith of a Christian that God is big enough to love everyone.

There was one spot in North London that could always fill me with doubt. I could see hundreds and hundreds of little houses in serried ranks. How could God know and love the human bees that swarmed there? Similarly New York in rush hour (or does it only *seem* harder and faster than London?), or some of the groups of skyscrapers that are human homes. I am bound to confess that the limitation I'm tempted to put on God is my own limitation.

I marvel at the person with a vast ability to keep up with innumerable friends. That same schoolfriend's father who prayed at some length before breakfast, but who, even a child knew, loved God and his fellows – he used to write nearly a thousand personal letters every Christmas. Hugh Redwood never broadcast without a list of names or initials somewhere on his script – the people of whom he was thinking especially, in the context of what he was saying.

The mother of a large family may be just as distressed by the loss of one of her children, as is the mother of one or two – perhaps even more so. Indeed is not this the secret about the exercise of love, that its capacity is increased by use? 'The man who has will be given more, till he has enough and to spare.' (Matthew 25: 29) And if, as I believe, all love originates in the 'stuff' of God, who is love, and if the capacity to love grows with its exercise, the vastness of the capacity to love, of perfect love, is infinitely vast, and to touch the hem of his garment is a revolutionizing experience. We cannot even try to think towards infinity without a sense of growing de-personalization. But that is because our ability to love is so limited, limited mostly to people we can see around us – limited sometimes by the fact that we can see them, and don't quite like what we see and want them to be different. Indeed an integral part of our very imperfect loving is that we have our own selfish pattern and mould into which we want people to fit if we are to go on loving them. And part of their trouble and ours is that the more we say we love them the harder we try to push them into our mould. We even blackmail those nearest, and, we say, dearest, to us: 'you know it upsets me if you do this' may not be a real reason for doing differently: sometimes illness is used as a sort of control lever on another life. But it isn't love that does this, but a desire for power. The God who has all power does not use it that way. He delegates power to us. He uses his power to give us freedom – freedom to choose his way or any other way. But if we choose his way, that is the same thing as choosing his love as the thing to live by.

It's a difficult thing to choose, because it is bound to make us and our way of life entirely different. And most of us want to stay as we are, or at least to work ourselves into our own preconceived pattern for ourselves and our future. We sing 'Nearer my God, to Thee, nearer to Thee' with great fervour and devotion. I'm not suggesting we are humbugs, but I'm sure we haven't worked out the implications of those words. Long before Jesus the old Hebrews saw something of the implication of proximity to perfection. They knew they couldn't stand it. They said 'no man can look on God and live'. So when godliness was being demonstrated, it had to be veiled in ordinariness with the sawdust of daily work. Occasionally something extraordinary broke through, so that looking back through perhaps half a century, John was able to say 'We beheld his glory'. But that was being wise after the event. Some were said to have seen angels heralding his birth; some by the touch of his hand or of the hem of his garment found 'magic'. Three disciples were claimed to have seen the glory break through in dazzling brightness so that his very clothes glistened; some said they heard God speak to him, but others said it was thunder; some were sure they saw the hand of God working through him, but others said he was in league with the devil.

I think the total of evidence for his being the revelation of God is overwhelming. But the evidence at one time seldom was or is overwhelming. Jesus even supplied the element of doubt himself sometimes so that no one needed to be overwhelmed. Both Jairus' daughter, and Lazarus, he described as 'sleeping'. You could make what you liked of that, though John reported that 'the chief priests resolved to do away with Lazarus, since on his account many Jews were going over to Jesus and putting their faith in him'. (John 12:10, 11).

Jesus occasionally took people aside to heal them or sent the crowd away. Once he used a known method of healing – he made clay of spittle. Always you could 'believe in him' or not. This looks like God's way of giving us freedom of choice. I believe it was and is God's way of giving us plenty of chances to make our choice. Was it not always God's way of freedom for us? To 'believe' or 'disbelieve', depends on the amount of discernment we are prepared to exercise – 'he that has ears, let him use them,' said Jesus on a number of occasions.

Have you thought of the number of stories, fact or fiction, that range round a very few themes? One of these is the very rich king with a beautiful daughter. He has to go to immense pains to ensure that she shall not be married for her money. This is a plot that seems almost eternal, perhaps because it *is* an eternal plot. I believe in a God who made this sort of plot; and that it took some plotting!

How was the creator of all that is, to ensure that his children would not love him cupboard-wise, for what they could get out of him? How could he be sure of being loved for himself, and not for a ticket to Heaven? No one, by being nicer, must be able to gain more of God's love and care. (Did it not seem to the writer of the epistle to the Hebrews that whom the Lord loves, he chastens?) Certainly the 'less nice' were not to feel that God was withholding his gifts from them. So, as Jesus pointed out, God gives his gifts, his sun and his rain, to the good and the bad, the just and the unjust.

Secondly it seemed that he needed to obscure himself behind his creation. You could see and share and enjoy the creation, you could experiment with it, misuse it, spoil and even destroy it, without so much as a nod to the creator. You could think you had earned it, won it, or made it yourself, and the real owner-creator would not disillusion you.

> 'I have been so great a lover.
> Filled my days so proudly with the splendour of love's dream'

wrote Rupert Brooke, and we could make a list comparable with his, of all the things in creation that we love. But what about people? The list of the people we love would not be long. There are so many that irritate us, or that we've grown tired of, or that we never could stand. . . .

To have been really 'so great a lover' is God's trouble. I believe that the pain and suffering and cross of Jesus were literally the outcome of loving like God. And that kind of loving must be consistently self-effacing to save it from being sought in greediness.

> 'He hides himself so wondrously
> As though there were no God' (Faber)

This seems to me to be the way of God with us his children. And it seems he has to do something similar with the wonders of his world. The 'inventor' is really a 'discoverer'; but because he is human he thinks he has invented something and God seems to let him (as when we propound a great idea and no one sees it as such – until years later someone brings it out as an idea of his own). Some of the great atheistic scientists have expressed a strong agnosticism when coming to the end of their life, which is a way of expressing reverence for an unknown factor. To be so clever as to think one knows all the answers is the height of irreverence. An expression of doubt about one's own omniscience may be the beginning of wisdom.

The argument for God's existence that I dislike least is Anselm's 'that than which no greater can be conceived'. But even this seems to depend on a person's ability to conceive of the inconceivable. There is the danger of its reducing God to a mere step beyond our comprehension. The Psalmist suggested that angels held that position. 'What is man? . . . Thou hast made him a little lower than the angels.' But the writer to the Hebrews says the Son who is 'the stamp of God's very being' is raised as far above the angels as the title he has inherited is superior to theirs'. (Hebrews 1 NEB).

If God were only a step beyond our comprehension then there would be some force in the cry we often put up – 'I can't understand. If there is a God, why doesn't he work the way I would – the way I think he should?' We would expect to be able to explain – nearly – why the gift of freedom must have pain and suffering in its wake; why perfection must be made remote by many imperfections; why love and truth and goodness and peace must, in the setting of freedom, have antitheses; why beings of character (which one supposes is another way of describing the Divine image stamped on us), can't be produced in, and remain in, a garden of Eden.

We would do it so differently. To begin with, to save unnecessary suffering, we would *make* people be decent to one another. And there in one blow goes our human freedom, our human privilege of being as inhuman – or as godlike – as we will.

Perhaps to try to work out the implications of how we would do it, would reduce us to size. 'Why does God allow it?' is the perpetual question of those who have discovered that doing what God doesn't allow has brought its natural consequence. But it is also the question of those who, like Job, expect their known measure of right living and keeping of the rules to produce a fair return of comfort and security. And such is the breadth of our freedom that we can choose to break all God's rules. But why should *I*, and how should *anyone*, claim to know God's rules?

Isn't this one of the things the Bible is for? It sets out what people thought to be the rules of life, and shows which worked, and which were only a temporary palliative. For example, when social justice was an unknown factor in Babylon, a man was valued for his property or his status – a slave had neither. So if a man of substance knocked out a poor man's eye, a bit of silver could be given for compensation. But if a poor man knocked out a rich man's eye, then the poor man's eye must be knocked out. So the Hebrew 'eye for an eye and a tooth for a tooth' regardless of status, was a great step forward. But the law was not brought to perfection – fulfilment – till Jesus. He said, 'It has been said of old time, an eye for an eye and a tooth for a tooth, but I say to you, love your enemies.'

Within the family, within the great family of the Hebrews, because they believed themselves peculiarly God's people, men began to grow up in their ideas of social justice; that's why Amos the great eighth century prophet of social justice was so horrified that a man could sell one of his own countrymen for a pair of shoes. But even 800 years later, the disciples of Jesus were told to try out their mission first on their own countrymen, in case they might be tempted to call down fire from heaven on inherited enemies. Later on they graduated to the idea of a mission to all the world.

So the heightening concept of social justice, learned first within the nation, could be seen by a prophet here and there to be a step towards God's plan for the inter-relationship of all people. 'Am I my brother's keeper?' Cain's question that comes near the beginning of the first book of the Bible, is being answered all the way through. You can see what happens when people practise social injustice and international injustice. To love God and love your neighbour makes a power of difference. I believe in a God whose plan is for the good of all his children.

And when one has said all this, what a vast impertinence it all is.

57

But because I believe in a God with a sense of humour (and not only because he created ducks), I believe he is lovingly amused at my impertinence – like parents with very small bumptious children –, not angry about it.

Here is this speck of life in an immeasurable universe daring to try to say something about the value and purpose behind the immeasurableness. If I were a sinless creature, perhaps I would not dare to do it. Something of the egotism of my fallen state, as it is called, helps me. The fact that I am conceited and big-headed and self-centred makes me bold to talk about God – as if I knew, as if I were always there, as if his plan was laid before me. (Shades of Job and the questions that came to him – 'Where wast thou when I laid the foundations of the earth?')

But again my egotism asserts itself; it some sense the plan *is* laid before me. This is my belief that 'he who made the stars made me', and made me able to contemplate the stars, and made me able to decide that the stars can't contemplate me. I even have the effrontery to believe that he has called me to a particular job in life. I spent some time doing other things and trying to think that giving my spare time to God was really enough; but that didn't work. 'I fled him down the night and down the days', but always he was there. And I had to give in, and for me that meant going to school again to learn how to be a minister. And each tentative, somewhat doubtful step led on to another until the doubt about that particular issue dwindled away.

But there were new problems to be faced. Did I believe in a God who gave me an exciting, driving sense of vocation, and gave a lot of other people jobs – sometimes dull monotonous jobs. Where now is the centenarian's philosophy that everyone is first with God? This sort of favouritism might well be yet another divisive factor among the children of men, and break the rule of 'no favourites' that Jesus stressed. What was the vocation God offered, and did he only offer it to the few? And even if it was tremendously important to me, would it not seem more important to many people that there should be someone to un-stop their drains or price the goods in the super-market? I remembered that it was mostly in quite ordinary events shared by a lot of people that God had 'called' me. For instance, those sermons I heard that seemed to demand a response in service had been preached to a whole congregation. Oh vanity! I even ascertained later that the preacher had no conscious sense of directing his words to a particular person. (Indeed one learns early in the Ministry never to do this. It always misfires!) Of the people who heard these particular sermons, maybe many responded to God's call to the vocation; but if the whole congregation had volunteered for the Ministry, they might well have been suspected of mass hysteria: What is our vocation? Is it not to accept the privilege of being a child of God and work out his plan for us? I believe his plan is there – to accept or reject. But the God I believe in takes great trouble to veil what he wants, so that free will can be real. And just as children in one family may, or more probably may not, follow one profession or trade, so God's family needs many members following various professions, trades, 'jobs' – but all are called to be one family and share in the responsibility for all.

The God I believe in calls all his children and suffers in the suffering of those who choose evil instead of good and hate instead of love, just as Jesus suffered in his earthly life because God's way was rejected.

We see in the Bible that there was a whole nation that called itself God's chosen people. In the history of those times we can read (outside the Bible) of another nation whose king saw for his people a similar relationship with one god. But the king was killed in battle while he was still very young. So his people decided his ideas must have angered the gods and they returned to their polytheism for safety's sake! They hoped to placate all the vengeful jealous, spiteful images they called gods.

But am I sure my idea of God is the right idea? No, of course I'm not. But at least it is vested in Jesus whom eyes saw and hands handled, though even those who were as close as that to him misunderstood him. John, one of the closest disciples, said, 'Master, we saw a man driving out devils in your name, and as he was not one of us, we tried to stop him.' Jesus said, 'Do not stop him; no one who does a work of divine power in my name will be able in the same breath to speak evil of me. For he who is not against us is on our side.'

God is so great we are bound to 'make his love too narrow, with false limits of our own' – as John did. So faith is always an adventure.

My faith has as its keystone my belief in God's plan for us, and in his willingness to go on offering it to us – over against all other plans, in such a way that we still can choose all the other plans, and in such a way that we are free to make our choice for ourselves.

> Choose for us, God: nor let our weak preferring
> Cheat our poor souls of good thou hast designed;
> Choose for us, God: thy wisdom is unerring,
> and we are fools and blind – (W. H. Burleigh, 1812-71)

may be good as a confession, but bad as a petition. If what God wills for us is perfection, his choice for us is already made – is eternally made. It is established by his nature. But we still cling to imperfection. And God does not overrule our will to imperfection – but goes on offering the best to people who like to pretend they know best. It makes them feel big and important (like breaking windows and slashing railway carriage seats) to be getting their own way against God.

Anyway, perfection is so big and far away I need something more frivolous, more light-hearted. And there's one of the mistakes about my belief in God. It's meant to make me light-hearted. Jesus said I was meant to become as a little child.

So forgive me, God, this effort to describe your incredible and indescribable greatness. At least I believe you are great enough and humble enough not to mind – and perhaps to be amused.

THOMAS CORBISHLEY, S.J.

was born in Preston, 1903, and educated at the Jesuit College, Preston. He joined the Society of Jesus, 1919, and studied at Campion Hall, Oxford, 1926-30 (First in Mods and First in Greats). Ordained 1936. Master of Campion Hall, 1945-58. Superior of Farm Street, 1958-1966. Lecturer, preacher, broadcaster, active in ecumenical work.

Publications: Roman Catholicism, Religion is Reasonable, Ronald Knox, The Priest, The Contemporary Christian. *Contributed to* The Catholic Commentary on the Bible, Religion in the Modern World *and numerous Journals.*

THOMAS CORBISHLEY

In this questioning, sceptical, religionless age, it must sound almost incredibly naive and unadventurous to declare that not only do I believe in God, but I always have and, barring some psychological catastrophe, it looks certain that I will continue to do so to the end of my days. For me, the reality of God is so much the very fabric of my thinking, the very basis of my whole way of life that the denial of that reality would be tantamount to intellectual suicide, a total disruption of the pattern of my activities. At the same time, it is necessary to assert at the outset of this analysis that my conviction about this Reality is not the outcome of a passive acceptance of a doctrine imposed on me from outside: it is the resultant of a strenuous and uninterrupted active response to the successive experiences of a life which has been lived in a milieu that has certainly been intellectually challenging and emphatically demanding.

It is, of course, true that, having been born into a devout Roman Catholic family, I accepted the idea of God along with a whole host of other notions – about politics, history, art, manners, social values of various kinds, including a firm conviction about the superiority of the British way of life and the endless detail of family relationships. It is equally true that the regular practice of Roman Catholic ritual and devotion was as much a part of life as support for the local football team and the routine of education. An important part of the strength of such religious development was precisely that it was taken for granted as the normal thing – accepted not only by my own family, but by my friends and their families, and so on.

To the unsympathetic reader this will all sound like so much indoctrination, a subtler form of brain-washing. Yet it is surely relevant that the world in which I grew up – that remote Lancashire world of the Edwardian era – is seen, in dim retrospect, as so different from the world of my maturity that the conventional psychological explanation seems to me totally inadequate. It is true that I retain a certain nostalgic devotion to that same football club – though my boyhood heroes are as remote as Francis Thompson's Hornby and Barlow –, but all the ideas I accepted in those early years have come under rigid scrutiny, not excepting my ideas about God. For whilst my convictions about the reality of God have deepened and strengthened with the years, it is because, all along, they have been tested against my widening experience and have been enriched by the very processes which have enabled me to arrive at a comprehensive view of life – a view that is coherent, intellectually satisfying and capable of standing up to every sort of pressure. This may sound like a boast. It is no more than a humble statement of a great good fortune for which I remain ever grateful.

One of the many dicta attributed to Jesuits in general and Ignatius Loyola in particular, is the one that goes something like 'Give me a boy for the first seven years of his life and you can have him for the rest'. Not only is the authenticity of this remark belied by the common practice of the Society of Jesus, which never, in fact, undertakes the education of the young until they have reached at least Prep school age; its truth, one would have thought, is belied by experience. One important reason for the prevalence of disbelief, especially in late adolescence, is precisely that so many intelligent and critically-minded young men (and women) reject the simple presentation of religious ideas which may have been suited to the minds of children but can no longer be found acceptable by the maturing intelligence. Unless they are fortunate enough to be encouraged to recognize the need to rethink their religious ideas along with their other views about life, they may well come to see religious faith as a childish affair, to be rejected by the independent-minded adult.

Part of the great good fortune to which I have referred is that, at the time when my own mind was so maturing, I found myself in the company of men whose intellectual integrity was beyond question and whose sophisticated approach to the profoundest religious problems was both a stimulus and an encouragement. Gradually but inexorably I found myself facing up to questions posed by belief, not only in God but in the truths of the Christian faith. Having been brought up in a relatively unsophisticated, though by no means unintelligent family, I was blest at school by finding myself in the hands of men who, whilst sharing the beliefs in which I had been nurtured, were not content to let these remain unquestioned and passive, but demanded an intelligent and critical evaluation of them in the light of contemporary attitudes. This was half-a-century ago when the challenge of unbelief was neither so aggressive nor so organized as it is today. Yet we were made aware that belief was not something automatic and inevitable. It had to be thought about, discussed, possessed. I still recall the impact made on me by a reading of Milton's *Areopagitica*. 'I cannot praise a fugitive and cloistered virtue, unexercised and unbreathed . . .'

Moving on from school to the novitiate of the Society of Jesus, I found myself in the company of a group of young or youngish men, from every kind of social background and with a varied experience, which included, in some cases, several years of active warfare. The year was 1919 and, though I had myself been too young to be called up, a dozen or so of my fellow-novices had fought in France and elsewhere. One at least had been a prisoner-of-war. Any suggestion that we were a group of callow youths, passive clay to be moulded by a remorseless engine into unthinking submission to a dehumanizing system would have struck us as merely fatuous. Not only were we free to discuss amongst ourselves our own convictions; we were given more than enough time for self-scrutiny and for an examination of the foundations of the Christian faith on which our whole lives were to be built. Anyone who was not sure of himself was allowed, indeed encouraged, to leave. A number did so, and their departure was, in the nature of things, a challenge to our own integrity of purpose.

From the novitiate we moved on to the next stage of our training – a course of philosophy, based on the Scholastic system, but with considerable attention to modern theories. Hard things have been said about Scholasticism, and it has to be confessed that it can be presented in a mechanical and over-systematized way. The unadventurous and unquestioning can accept it passively, as a complete answer to every problem. For some it was a tedious exercise in unintelligent digesting of a number of prepared statements about metaphysical abstractions or ethical conundrums. But the more intelligent students could and did argue earnestly

E

and endlessly about the validity of the ideas which had been presented to us. We could read as widely as we liked in the works of philosophers both ancient and modern, though the emphasis was naturally on the positive content of the *philosophia perennis*.

For my own part, I came to the end of my course of philosophy feeling vaguely dissatisfied with the method of teaching, recognizing that it was hardly commensurate with the nature and scale of the problems it sought to discuss. But the interesting point for our immediate purpose is that this dissatisfaction had no apparent effect on the strength of my deepest convictions. The fact is, of course, that belief in God, although it has an important intellectual dimension is not exhausted by any purely intellectual analysis. Just as human love, rooted as it may be in social, intellectual and even biological factors, is nevertheless much more than an amalgam of these, so does belief in God depend on influences that cannot be reduced wholly to the dialectical or semantic. Leaving aside the influence of what the theologians call 'grace' (which, anyhow, does not operate without reference to natural causes), there are certain psychological ethical and social factors which cannot always be precisely analysed, but the effect of which is incontestable.

Certainly, in my own case, 'by some divine chance', the whole pattern of my life became increasingly meaningful in the light of my faith. Whether it was that the whole 'mechanism' of my life as a Jesuit – prayer and worship, fellowship in a common vocation, the sense of belonging to a high tradition – whether these 'strengthened' my faith in God or whether that faith gave deeper significance to my life, is not easy to analyse clearly. Perhaps it can best be described as a 'virtuous circle'. What is beyond cavil is that, at this time in particular, as my intellectual development was reaching its maturity, I could no more have questioned the existence of God than I could have doubted the love of my parents. The question just did not arise.

At least, the question did not arise as an anguishing experience. I was not unaware of the problems connected with God's 'being there' – problems which will call for discussion later. Nor was it that I have ever experienced, or thought I have experienced, what is called the 'felt presence of God'. Like most believers, probably, I have had moments of emotional 'religious experience'. But these

have never *mattered*. I have never used them to bolster up my
faith, which has, increasingly, been an unemotional matter-of-fact
affair, rather like one's conviction about the rationality of the universe or one's recognition of the importance of intellectual hon-
esty. I knew that many people questioned the existence of God.
I knew that many denied his existence. Nor did I question their
sincerity. It was just that such an attitude of mind would never
have made sense to me.

When I went up to Oxford to read Greats (and I did get two
Firsts: I state the fact because it is relevant) I was, of course, committed to asking all the inevitable questions connected with this
ground of my very being. My philosophy tutor was A. H. Smith
who had published a study of Kant and put me through an inten-
sive course of that undogmatic critic. I sat at the feet of Joseph
and Pritchard; I read widely in modern philosophy; I argued with
my fellows, whose intellectual ability I recognized and whose integrity I respected. I could even see the point of view of the agnostic. Indeed this very agnosticism in a curious way enriched
my faith, since it tied in with the whole idea of the *via negativa*,
which is such an important and fruitful element in the whole
Christian doctrine of God.

Perhaps this is an appropriate point at which to interject some
considerations about this aspect of our approach to God. Some
years ago, at the height of the anti-metaphyiscal attitude which
stemmed from logical positivism and went by the name of linguistic analysis, it was fashionable to ask the question: 'Can talk
about God have any meaning?' and answer it, of course, with a
resounding and emphatic negative. What such semantic exercises
never seemed to take into account was that they were, in fact,
(like the Kantian *Kritik* itself) only a poor variety of an attitude of
mind which had had highly respectable, *believing* exponents.
From Augustine and the Pseudo-Denys, through Thomas
Aquinas and the medieval mystics to John of the Cross and many
others, a whole host of convinced Christians had emphasized the
total inadequacy of human language, human imagery, human concepts as applied to God. But, as they saw it, this was due not to
the unreality of God but to the inadequacy of man. They knew
that, just as the artist and the poet are conscious of an inability

to express their vision, without thereby denying the reality of the vision –

('fancies that broke through language and escaped'

are, *in a sense* 'meaningless' because they are too great *for* language) – so, by definition, no language or imagery derived from experience of the created (and all human language is such) can possibly apply to the Uncreated. Even Kant, at least by implication, admitted the existence of a noumenal world, even though it was inaccessible, directly, to the human mind, bound as this is, of its nature, to the phenomenal order.

The unexpected outcome, then, of my Greats course was that, having gone up to Oxford feeling a certain dissatisfaction with the traditional Scholastic approach to philosophical problems, I came down with a heightened respect for its combination of faith in the powers of human reason with a recognition of the limits of that same reason. It is all very well to write off as non-existent anything which cannot be clearly stated and adequately conceptualized. But, even at the level of ordinary experience, such an attitude would impoverish human life unbearably. The profoundest human relationships, the sublimest aesthetic experiences, everything in fact, which enriches and ennobles man's journey through the world – all this is beyond the range of syllogistic reasoning or propositional statement. The lover is literally incapable of expressing to anyone else the unique quality that makes his love what it is and nothing else. He can hint at it, rhapsodize about it, describe its effects. He cannot communicate it in words. There is an important sense in which talk about it, if not meaningless, is at least a betrayal of it.

At the same time, even if it is not possible to state in any adequate way what is meant by believing in God, it may be necessary at times to justify one's faith. (This, I take it, is the point of the famous Five Ways of Thomas Aquinas. Since he concludes his five arguments by saying: '... this everyone understands to be God' or '... to this everyone gives the name of God' and so on, he is clearly talking to believers, not trying to convince unbelievers.) The simple point I want to make here is that it has always seemed to me to be more *reasonable* to accept the existence of God than to question or deny it. Nor do I mean by this anything like Pascals's view that, on balance, it pays to believe. For me the existence of God is closely bound up with the rationality of the world, with man's conviction, 'that somehow the Right is the Right', with his readiness to dedicate himself to the service of some cause from which he personally derives no immediate benefit, which may, indeed, cost him his life.

Again, this does not mean that God is a kind of Public Utility, that, 'if he did not exist it would be necessary to invent him', which is another form of *expedit esse deos et ut expedit esse putemus*.[1] What it does mean is that all these convictions point to an ultimate and absolute Ground without which these ideas would be just hanging in the air, doomed to final frustration, essentially pointless and illusory. Nor will it do to retort that these things are worth-while because they help to promote the onward march of mankind, to ensure the survival of the tribe or something like that. This is only to push the matter one stage further back. Faith in Progress is an excellent thing. But Progress, by definition, is not an end in itself; it is intelligible only in terms of that towards which we are progressing, or striving to progress. So we are brought up against another puzzle, to which there seems to be no answer on any purely empirical system.

What is it that inspires the Humanist, the Marxist, the Utilitarian philosopher no less than the Christian reformer 'to scorn delights and live laborious days' in order to achieve some benefit for future generations? In the words of the cynic: 'What has posterity done for me?' In purely this-world terms there is no satisfactory answer. There is, of course, a partial answer. It is that we all – unless we are hopelessly selfish – recognize that human beings, simply *qua* human beings, have a claim on our sympathy, our generosity, our help. That is the way we are made.

Precisely. 'That is the way we are made.' Again, the answer of the man who holds that we are made that way by some process of Natural Selection, operating blindly but inexorably to produce ever higher and higher types, seems to me hopelessly thin and superficial. Clearly the whole theory of Evolution is of the greatest value in studying the long history of man's development and only the nervous bigot would seek to discredit its importance. But, try

[1] 'It is expedient that the gods should exist, and in accordance with expediency let us suppose that they do'.

as I may, I just cannot see how the biological processes which have gone to the development of man's physical structure, including especially the convolutions of his brain, can provide the total explanation of the origins of man's religious and moral ideas. In the naked struggle for survival, the notions of unselfishness and sympathy for the weak, the pursuit of beauty, the cultivation of the things of the mind (except in a purely utilitarian sense) seem to have no place at all.

And here again, just as the linguistic analyst has borne witness to one aspect of the Christian notion of God, so has the evolutionary scientist helped to deepen our appreciation of the way in which God's creative power operates. Gone are the days when we thought of God as tinkering with the universe from outside, intervening from time to time, now to produce life, now to inject human souls, occasionally to perform a miracle in answer to prayer, or for some inscrutable purpose of his own. Without falling into the mistake of accepting the (essentially irreligious) notions of the pantheist who would identify God with his universe, we are beginning to take seriously the teaching of some of the great religious thinkers of the past, who have asserted that God is closer to us than we are to ourselves.

But then we come back to the ultimate puzzle raised by our thinking about God. As Kant insisted, Space and Time are forms of our thought, valid only for this phenomenal order, irrelevant to the noumenal world of ultimate reality. In this, he is doing little more than to elaborate the traditional teaching about God's eternity, as described in a classic statement by Boethius: *Interminabilis vitae tota simul et perfecta possessio* – 'the utter and complete comprehension of life without end in one simultaneous act'. It is because the whole of our experience is of succession and of discreteness (whether in space or time) that we cannot imagine, can hardly begin to conceive of an order of reality that is not so limited. Yet, just as Kant was driven to postulate that sort of ground of the phenomenal order, so the believer finds himself accepting a Being towards which all his experience points, even whilst he becomes increasingly aware that he himself is totally unable, of himself, to say anything about it that is literally true.

Yet he is satisfied that this world of Space and Time is, paradoxically, the realm in which the Godhead – spaceless and timeless – manifests himself. Because the profoundest speculations of the most subtle philosopher are just as inadequate to express the nature of God as are the simple stammerings of the unlettered believer, he is not disconcerted (except perhaps aesthetically) by traditional religious imagery and language. Equally, he recognizes that theology's claim to have, so to say, 'cornered' God, has done something of a disservice even to religious truth. He knows that truth, from whatever source it comes, is but a further revelation of the inexhaustible fullness of truth, wholly realized in the Divine Mind, fragmentarily grasped by created intelligence. If you ask him, then, why he believes in such an inscrutable reality, his answer might go something like this.

In the first place, man finds himself a feature of a total reality which conditions his being and controls his development. In the sphere of intellectual activity, he does not bring truth into being. He discovers it. He may make it more comprehensible to himself by his statement of it, but he knows that his success depends on the measure in which he accepts the laws governing his mental processes, just as, in the material order, he can only develop the resources of nature by using them in accordance with what they are. Moreover, he finds that, from the beginning of his conscious life, he is impelled to ask questions, in particular the question, Why? He knows that things do not just happen; there is an explanation for any event, whether or not he can discover it. But he wants to discover it; he is dissatisfied if he encounters some detail, some incident which looks like a sheer accident. In an increasingly mechanized world, he is even less inclined to leave things to chance. Machines must be made more and more precise, the laws of mathematics and physics studied with increasing sophistication, breakdowns must be traced back to their causes.

In other words, reason and law are the very basis of his life and of the world in which he finds himself. In the words of Plato, the *logos* within him corresponds to a *logos* outside him. This is why human life is possible at all. But the logos is not 'outside' him in any purely spatial sense. On the contrary, whilst it is 'other', it is also something with which he is in intimate association, something which assists, supports, encourages him. Or, to put it in another way, he is compelled, logically, to recognize the existence of an order of reality on which he is dependent and yet to which he is, in some way, akin. This enables him to accept without any difficulty the statement in the book of Genesis that God 'created man in his own image and likeness'. Recognizing that he is in the presence of a reality that is superior to him in every imaginable way, he is satisfied that this Reality can best be thought of as Personal – with all that that means of Wisdom, Creative Power and Love – though without the limitations which he is all too conscious of in his own personal relationships.

Nor is he dismayed by the suggestion that man has made God in his own image. As we have seen, it is not possible for man to think of God except in terms derived from his own experience. At the same time, he knows that (to use Bultmann's term) it is necessary to demythologize his language, to accept the simple psychological fact that, all his life, he will be out-growing his previous notions about this God who is at once the explanation of man's own nature, with all its capacities, and is yet transcendent, independent, in Himself wholly *other*. Yet this very otherness is not a quality that divides; it is an essential constituent of a relationship. For the relationship of love demands that the beloved shall be wholly other, independent, existing in her (or his) own right precisely in order that the relationship may be a real communion.

If he is inclined, by temperament or professional concern, to intellectualize his ideas about God, he will find the balance corrected if he is fortunate enough to experience a complete human love. If he has ever come to find the centre of his interest in someone other than himself, if he has ever really appreciated that Copernican revolution which makes him think of himself as a planet rather than as a sun, this will enrich his attitude towards God-as-Love. Once he has come to think that, at the deepest level, reality is self-giving, this begins to make sense of a whole complex of ideas – from the initial act of Creation, manifested in this universe, prepared for man, given to man for his use and enjoyment; through the idealism of the philanthropist, the humanist, the loyal servant; through the self-sacrifice of husband for wife, of mother for child; through the dedicated zeal of the great benefactors of mankind – the research scientist, the authentic scholar, the genuine artist, the whole race of all-but anonymous individuals who work in obscurity to improve the human lot;

on to every instance of men and women who have been prepared to lay down their lives for whatever cause they believed in. Without wishing to maintain that in all, or perhaps in any, of these cases less worthy motives have never been present, the fact remains that the history of man has been enlightened and enriched by such a host of generous and high-minded spirits that some explanation, almost one might say some justification, of their conduct is demanded. It is surely found most satisfactorily in the view that man is indeed created in the image and likeness of Love hypostatized.

Which brings us, of course, to the inevitable question about the existence of evil in a world created by Love. Have I never revolted against the horrors that infest this world – the loathsome diseases, the natural catastrophes, the infamies practised by men on their fellows, the ugliness of death, the promise of youth wantonly destroyed, all the long tale of human misery and degradation and heart-break? Where does my faith in God fit into such a picture?

Well, first of all let me assure the sceptic that I do feel all this problem so acutely that, but for my faith in God, I should certainly despair, that it is only my faith which makes it possible for me to remain full of hope and enthusiasm in the face of every kind of frustration and disappointment. What is, it seems to me, highly relevant in all this matter is the surely significant fact that we all of us – believers or not – are for ever talking about the problem of Evil; we never talk about the problem of Good. Yet if the world were simply the product of the interplay of unintelligent and unsympathetic forces, why on earth should we be puzzled or perplexed by the fact of suffering as though it constituted a *moral* problem? Naturally we resent suffering in those near and dear to us; their suffering is ours. But, as to whether we suffer or not, this is really only a matter of chance. If, when catastrophe befalls, I exclaim: Why should this happen to me? or even why should it happen at all?, I ought to be logical enough to ask precisely the same question when things go well. We do not, as a rule, ask this question because, in our heart of hearts, we believe that to be happy, to be comfortable, to succeed, to enjoy the society of our loved ones is, or should be, the *normal* thing.

The believer, like the unbeliever, is grateful when things go well. But the believer, unlike the unbeliever, is in the happy (and human) position of being grateful to Somebody. When on the other hand, things go wrong, he does not just indulge in blind resentment. Believing as he does in the ultimate rationality of the world, he is satisfied that suffering is not just a gigantic error, absurd in the scheme of things. There must be some way of justifying it, of reconciling it not merely with the fact of God's existence, but with the reality of his love.

Three considerations, stemming from his faith, help him to make some sort of sense of this situation. In the first place, he realizes that, just as Time does take the sting out of much of man's sorrows, so his ability to look at terrestrial events *sub specie aeternitatis* does give him a sense of proportion. He recalls that some of the most agonizing experiences of his life, when recollected in tranquility, are seen to have resulted in an enlargement and an enrichment of his personality in a way that perhaps nothing else could. *Souffrir passe; avoir souffert ne passe pas* is an apophthegm which enshrines a valuable lesson.

Secondly, he tries to bear in mind the obvious fact that a sizeable proportion of man's suffering springs from man's wilfulness, stupidity, greed, cruelty, especially the manic frenzy which seizes on men who find themselves in positions of what they think of as absolute power. He can see that such conduct is the obverse of man's responsibility for the destiny of the human race. For better, or for worse, God has endowed man with this dignity, so that he is a free agent, with all that that implies. The more fully he recognizes the nature of his stewardship, that is to say, the more he tries to manage his affairs in the light of the prudence, the generosity, the selfless love which are sufficiently clear as guiding principles of conduct, the greater will be the total well-being of mankind. Seeing this much as an empirical fact, he is prepared to accept the view, traditional at least in the Judaeo-Christian tradition, that all evil stems in the end from the recalcitrance of a creation unwilling to accept its creatureliness.

Thirdly, since the problem is not wholly, perhaps not primarily a purely intellectual one, charged as it is with such emotional overtones, he is helped above all by the Christian doctrine of the Incarnation, which assures him that, far from remaining aloof and unconcerned, God has involved himself in the human situation, with all its triumphs and failures. The profound mystery of the redemptive suffering of Christ teaches him that, whilst the folly, the jealousy, the weakness, the cruelty of human beings produced such terrible results in the torture and execution of a wholly innocent human individual, the ultimate outcome of this whole story is the assurance of a total restoration of all things 'in Christ'. Christ's sufferings, his physical pain and his mental agony, which, taken by themselves might seem pointless and wantonly cruel, are seen as the very antidote to all the world's evils. How this can be no one would hope to explain clearly. But the doctrine does give the believer ground for reassurance and hope.

The other common explanation for the atheist's rejection of God or the agnostic's suspension of belief springs undoubtedly, as often as not, from a rejection of unworthy presentations of 'God'. We have seen how the adolescent often rejects the religious ideas which have been given to him in childhood, because they are childish presentations. At a more sophisticated level, men not unnaturally reject notions about God which were acceptable in a less civilized society or in an age which knew little or nothing of scientific method as we understand it. The modern physicist has given up phlogiston as an explanation of combustion; he has substituted another explanation, another 'picture'. But the underlying reality he is trying to explain remains unaltered. So is it with our notions about God. We must develop an increasingly sophisticated way of thinking about him, not just reject him outright because we cannot accept other people's way of thinking, talking about him. Perhaps Wittgenstein may be allowed to have the last word: 'If you cannot express something, better not talk about it.'

Yet, that will not quite do either. However inscrutable the mystery of the divine nature may be, the reality of him is so tremendous that one is impelled, however stammeringly, to emphasize it. Possibly a poet – and a Jesuit poet at that – may be quoted to round off this analysis.

> Ground of Being and Granite of it, past all
> Grasp God, throned behind death
> With a sovereignty
> That heeds but hides, bodes by abides.

RUPERT E. DAVIES

was born in London in 1909 *and educated at St Paul's School, Balliol College, Oxford (where he was a Classical Scholar), Wesley House, Cambridge, and the University of Tübingen. At Oxford he took a First in Honour Moderations, and a Second in Greats; at Cambridge a First in Theology. He was Chaplain of Kingswood School, Bath, from* 1935 *to* 1947, *and ordained to the Methodist Ministry in* 1937. *From* 1947 *to* 1952 *served in Methodist Circuits in Bristol; from* 1952 *to* 1967 *he was Senior Tutor at Didsbury College, Bristol, and in* 1967 *became Principal of Wesley College, Bristol. He is a Recognized Teacher in the University of Bristol.*

He is Convener of the Faith and Order Committee of the Methodist Church and a member of the Anglican-Methodist Unity Commission. He is a member of the Faith and Order Commission of the World Council of Churches and of its Working Committee. He has been a Select Preacher to the University of Cambridge. He was on the Bristol Education Committee for ten years, and Secretary to the Governors of Kingswood School for nearly twenty years.

His books include: The Problem of Authority in the Continental Reformers; Praying Together; Studies in I Corinthians; Methodists and Unity; *and* Methodism. *He joined with R. Newton Flew to edit* The Catholicity of Protestantism; *and is co-editor with E. Gordon Rupp of the official history of the Methodist Church in Great Britain.*

He married Margaret Price Holt in 1937, *and they have five children (one adopted), and an increasing number of grandchildren.*

RUPERT E. DAVIES

I am not religious by temperament. Worship and prayer do not come easily to me. In fact, they require a considerable effort of concentration if they are to have much meaning for me. I am not prone to what are called religious experiences. There have been occasions in my life when I have been directly conscious of what I believe to be the peace of God. Others, I suppose, might interpret such occasions in other ways. I hold them to be of divine origin because I already believe in a God who from time to time makes himself personally known to those who trust in him, and, indeed, not infrequently to those who do not. But they have not given me that absolute certainty of the presence of God which some people, more religiously disposed than I, seem to have. So nobody, I think, could plausibly maintain that I am a Christian because of the way in which I am made. On the contrary, both by nature and training, I have a strong tendency to question and criticize what other people ask me to believe.

My upbringing was Christian without being particularly pious. My parents were very busy people, but not too busy to give me the care and affection which I needed. They set before me a very high standard of devotion to the service of the community, which, I hope, I have never entirely forgotten. I owe a great deal to my brother, much older than myself, who during my adolescence led a Bible Class which I naturally joined. The Bible Class very strictly lived up to its name, and its basis was a type of theology which included the dogma that the Bible is the infallible Word of God. But, as taught by my brother and his assistants, it did not clamp any rigid or exclusive views or attitudes on to me, and my own theological opinions have developed quite naturally from what I was taught as a boy, without any violent revulsions or 'going to the other extreme'. I cannot say that St Paul's School, though it is doubtful whether any other school could have given me a more exacting intellectual training, contributed very much to my Christian development.

It was my brother who brought me into the life of the Church of which I am now a minister, it was Oxford which confirmed me in my membership of it. This was a rather unusual thing to happen, since there were only forty-eight known Methodists in the whole student body in the years that I was up. But several of them were men and women of great intelligence and insight, and our leader and pastor during most of my time was Harold Roberts,[1] in whose company I learned that frank and searching discussion of the most fundamental doctrines is part of the essence of Christian faith. We argued interminably, and passed through many phases of Christian theology in a short time. But in the Long Vacation we descended on some harmless town, industrial or market, and expounded the Christian Faith to anyone who came to listen. This activity may not have added many converts to the Christian Church, but it certainly showed us that what cannot be communicated is not necessarily worth believing, and incidentally exposed us to all the taunts that were being levelled against the Church during the days of the Great Depression. It also opened my eyes to social and human problems of which I had not previously been aware, and gave a permanent slant to my political opinions.[2]

It was in Oxford Methodism, too, that I first met my wife, and the common experience of Oxford itself and of the Methodism which flourished (yes, flourished) within its walls is certainly an integral part of all that unites us.

So my faith developed gradually, not by crises and revolutions. I can compress a long process into a statement of faith by saying that, with a fair knowledge of other views of the world, and a proper respect for them, I find in Jesus of Nazareth the very meaning of human existence. His impact on me is such that I cannot possibly understand him in purely human terms; and when I see what he has done to millions of other people and to the whole course of human history, a purely human interpretation of him becomes absurd. (I shall say more of this later.) In the Gospels, he meets me with an offer which I must either accept

[1] For many years Principal of Richmond College, Surrey; Methodist Chairman of the Anglican-Methodist Unity Commission.

[2] One of the towns we visited was Blackburn, where the unemployed formed 32 per cent of the total working population.

or reject, with demands upon me which I must meet or deny, but only a coward can evade, and with a way of thought and life which I cannot treat lightly, but either allow to penetrate to the depths of my being or fling away resolutely and completely. In other words, he makes a total, personal appeal to my total being. If I respond with feeling alone, or with reason alone, or with will alone, or with anything short of a total commitment, I do not take him seriously. It must be all or nothing. As Freisler, the President of the People's Court which tried the failed conspirators against Hitler of July 20, 1944, screamed out in his tirades against one of the accused: 'Only in one respect does National Socialism resemble Christianity: we demand the whole man.'

It is through Jesus Christ that I believe in God. It is quite possible that I should believe in the existence of God if I were not a Christian. If we take the whole broad sweep of human experience, and do not limit ourselves to purely philosophical considerations, the hypothesis that God exists and is the Creator of the universe is a highly plausible one. But I should be left with a whole series of questions about the character and purpose of God which would admit of no answer, and I doubt very much whether a bare belief in the existence of God would greatly affect my manner of life. But because of Jesus – that is, because I have committed myself to him and all that he stands for – I believe certain quite definite things about God. I believe that he is other and greater than the universe, a personal being of infinite power, wisdom and goodness. I am well aware that to call him 'personal' opens me to the charge of naiveté, for it seems to degrade God to a human level of existence. But I am careful not to call him a 'person', which would so degrade him, but 'personal', which is the least unsatisfactory way of speaking of a God who treats me as a person and who encourages me to address him personally. Of course, he is far more than personal, but he is at least personal. He is the Creator of all that is. To say this, passes no judgment whatever on matters which lie within the competence of the scientist, not the theologian – for instance, whether energy is 'eternal', or came into existence by some kind of 'big bang' or other catastrophic event. The Christian doctrine of creation is not a doctrine of how things happened, but of the relation which permanently exists between the world and God, a relation of complete dependence, so that if God (*per impossibile*) were to cease to will the existence of the universe, it would not exist. The universe is derivative, not self-existent. The stories of creation in Genesis are the source of much misunderstanding to the modern mind. They were put in historical, quasi-scientific form for those for whom they were written, not for us. They are, in the proper sense, myths of creation, designed to indicate the simple and profound truth that the world and man depend on God alone for their origin and continuance.

God is in control of the universe, as Sovereign and Father, and he controls it for the benefit of those who live in it. Christians are in the habit of saying: God is our Father, and they have excellent authority for saying it. A good deal of play has been made by some of the linguistic philosophers of the fact that God is never seen to behave in the way in which human fathers, at their best, behave. He does not come to the rescue of a badly wounded man, or someone dying from a malignant growth – as, surely, a human father would in the case of his son or daughter, with the advantage that God, being God, could actually cure the patient. How then can we meaningfully call him 'Father'? When Jesus called God 'Father' he used the best word available to describe God's attitude to his creatures, and to his human creatures in particular. It was an especially good word for him to use, since fatherhood to the ancient Jew carried the meaning of both authority and benevolence in a way in which no word today does. Thus he was able to say in a single word that God exercises supreme authority and control, and at the same time works for the highest of all. When a modern Christian says: 'God is our Father', he means exactly this, but he has an advantage in understanding it which the first hearers of Jesus did not have: in the life and character of Jesus himself he sees the concrete expression of what fatherhood means. In other words, to call God 'Father' means that God's attitude to the world is the same as Jesus' attitude to the world. As Jesus loved all men, including the 'unthankful and the evil', and including also his murderers, so God loves all men, including the evil and the blasphemous, and those who, for good reasons or bad, spend their energy in denying his existence. As Jesus offered his friendship to all who came within his orbit, but wished for no response except in freedom, so God offers his grace to all, but has no use for coercion or indoctrination: men must obey him in love and freedom, or their obedience is that of a slave, and not of a son, and God wishes for sons, not slaves.

The scope of God's activity is not limited to human existence on this planet, though plainly he takes great interest in this, since he goes to so much trouble, and receives so many rebuffs, in creating it and sustaining it. If God is God, then he is eternal, unlimited by time or space. Or, perhaps better, he *is*. This fact puts quite a different complexion on the problem of evil from that which it usually bears. Christians are very well aware of the problem of evil, usually more aware of it than non-Christians. For if you believe in a God of love, the presence of so much evil in the world is a very serious difficulty to your faith. If you do not believe in a God of love, there is no problem of evil, except as something with which to taunt the Christians. You have, of course, the far more serious problem of *good* on your hands. If there is no God, or no God of love, it is very hard indeed to explain why there is so much good, in the form of design, knowledge, love, beauty, happiness, etc. In fact, no explanation has yet been offered.

But evil, both in the shape of wrongdoing on a small or large scale, and in the shape of undeserved illness and calamity, is an immense problem for Christians, and for anyone else who believes that the universe is in the hand of a benevolent power. We can say – and, I believe, rightly say – that since God has given us freedom of choice between good and evil we must suppose that he has also placed us in a world where the laws of cause and effect apply. If we could jump off the Clifton Suspension Bridge, and sometimes fall to the bottom, and sometimes be carried through the air in safety to another point on the bridge, this would be no kind of world for the exercise of true freedom. Freedom involves the power to set on foot a series of dire events. And we can thus explain a large proportion of the evil in the world, and do so quite consistently with belief in a God of love. But there is still a large residue of unexplained evil, consisting for the most part of natural disasters, but also including what seems to be the excess of pain inflicted on the innocent by the exercise of free choice on the part of the guilty. If God's activity is restricted to this world, it is hopelessly facile to say that 'everything will come right in the end', and that 'God's will is inscrutable'. But if we hold that the scope of God's activity is eternity, and that he goes on bringing us to maturity even when our life on earth is over, then we can begin to make some sense of the sufferings which men are called on to endure. This is not to say, of course, that troubles here will be compensated by bliss hereafter, or that we need not work for the removal of evil since God will put everything right in the next world. On the contrary, since God's will is human maturity and freedom and justice, and since a great deal of pain is as liable to degrade as to ennoble the victim, those who take God's will seriously will work night and day to remove all the evil in the world that they can get their hands on. And there is no trace of a law of compensatory happiness in heaven, but only of the growth to freedom of those who trust in God.

I believe in the forgiveness of sins. I notice that quite a number of Christians today are reluctant to use the word 'sin' for fear of being suspected of taking too gloomy a view of human nature. It is true that the concept of sin has been confused in the past by too great a preoccupation with sex, and with ideas of 'original sin' and 'total depravity' which have suggested that there is nothing good in human nature and that all plans for human welfare this side of heaven are doomed to failure. But the abuse of an idea does not destroy its proper use. Man is capable of great good – his inventiveness seems to know no bound, and his moral qualities are considerable, especially in time of crises. But he has also a 'traitor streak' in his nature. He never quite achieves what he sets out to achieve, and the reason is usually that something goes wrong in personal relations, or that some inner desire or ambition gets out of hand. This is plainly true of individuals and communities alike. This is not really denied by anyone, and modern literature, which is far from being theological in general, is obsessed with what Christian theologians call 'sin', and others call 'meaninglessness' or 'failure to be authentic'. The Christian holds that the root of this is not moral, but spiritual, though the moral results may be the most obvious. Man is made for a life of personal relationship with God and his fellows. But our obstinate tendency to assert ourselves against what we know to be the will of God damages the relationship very early in life, and may in due course destroy it absolutely. From this breakdown follow the other evils of human existence, the 'sins', which are in fact the symptoms of 'sin', which is our alienation from God. This is what the doctrine of 'original sin' is about – not about some alleged past event which has condemned the whole human race ever since. Original sin is something in each of us; each of us is the 'Adam of his own soul', as an ancient Jewish writer put it. We are 'fallen creatures' – divided and pulled both ways by the good and evil in us. And the story of Adam, properly understood, tells us just that; it throws into sharp relief the contrast and the conflict between the voice of God, drawing us upward, and the voice of self, drawing us downward, and bluntly indicates that the usual result is the victory of the 'lower self', with its attendant evils. Adam, in fact, is Everyman, not the progenitor of the human race; and his story is our story.

But 'Original Sin' has another connotation. 'Sin' is not only, or chiefly, personal. It is also social. The human situation is not just that of isolated individuals, each carrying on his own personal struggle for freedom and integrity. It is also that of men and women living in communities, communities of all shapes and sizes, involved in each other's discoveries and successes, mistakes and failings. We are not born into, and we do not grow up in, a clean and innocent environment which offers each of us an entirely fresh start. Our world is already bedevilled by the crimes and errors of our predecessors and contemporaries before we take any active part in its life, just as it is illuminated by their wisdom and skill. Very rarely, if ever, in the whole course of our lives do we find ourselves in a situation in which we have a clear choice between what is wholly good and what is wholly evil. Of two courses before us each is partly good and partly bad in its consequences, and our choice is between the lesser and the greater good, or, more often, between the lesser and the greater evil. To campaign for Civil Rights in the Southern States of America involves incitement to violence, and injury and death for guiltless people; but to refrain from campaigning perpetuates a vast injustice for millions. The people who work and pray for peace make their living in a society which owes a good deal of such economic stability as it possesses to the successful waging of wars. It can easily happen that everyone in a particular country sincerely desires peace, and yet that country finds itself in a position in which war is inevitable. And badness (like goodness, only more so) is infectious, especially when 'mob psychology' comes into action. The men attending a football match may be, without exception, honest and peaceable men, good husbands and fathers, but something may happen on the field, like the apparently undeserved defeat of the home side, which will turn them into a howling mob, ready to tear the referee limb from limb. This also is Original Sin, perhaps nowadays most manifest of all on the roads of civilized countries.

Jesus made the forgiveness of sins the keynote of his message and of his life. The first effect of his personality was to awaken a consciousness of sin in people of different kinds, including respectable people who without him could easily have got away with the consciousness of their own rectitude. 'Depart from me, for I am a sinful man, O Lord,' said Peter. The second effect was that they asked for and obtained forgiveness. This gave rise to many objections. 'What right has this man to forgive sins? Surely this is God's prerogative.' The Christian view is that the forgiveness of sins is certainly God's prerogative – for 'sin', as we have seen, is always, basically, against God – and that Jesus had every right to exercise it, for he had the authority of God behind him. And they base this belief on what happened on, and as a result of, the Cross which was used as the instrument of his execution. He continued his policy of forgiveness to the bitter end, and prayed for the forgiveness of his murderers while they were actually murdering him: 'Father, forgive them, for they know not what they do.' Was this just quixotic, or the sign of Jesus' quite remarkable power of absorbing hostility without becoming hostile – or was it also effective? *Were* the murderers of Christ forgiven? Perhaps not those who perpetrated the crime of murdering him (apart from the centurion at the Cross, who recognized the greatness of Jesus); but since that time, and through all the succeeding ages, millions of men and women who started off by opposing what Jesus stood for, or by being sullenly indifferent to it, have 'changed their minds' (which is what 'repentance' means in the New Testament) when they have been told about the Cross of Jesus Christ, and have asked for and obtained the forgiveness which he offered there. And if it is asked how we know that they have been forgiven, the answer is that they have shown all the signs of forgiveness: they have turned from one way of life to another, inwardly as well as outwardly, and they have had that personal relation with God which previously was unknown to them. Thus we have good right to say that Jesus' offer of forgiveness – made constantly during his lifetime, and sealed by his unfaltering love on the Cross – was made on the authority of God himself.

Jesus was concerned mainly, if not exclusively, with the forgiveness of individual people. He was not in a position to exercise influence on the complications of organized society. Neither Emperor, nor Governor, nor High Priest, was among his audience. But there is an important sense in which he 'forgave' the 'sin of the world' as well as the sin of individuals. He brought together the nucleus of a society which was commissioned to serve the human race – its institutions and groupings, as well as its members – to the furthest limit of love and endurance, just as he had himself served his friends and his enemies. His Church was instructed to take in hand the purification of the whole of human life, to cleanse it from Original Sin (in its social aspect), not by lording it over human affairs, but by self-disregarding service to the community at all times. And if this process does not seem to have advanced very far since the time of Jesus, it has to be acknowledged that the Church, to its everlasting shame, has frequently betrayed its trust, not least in the matter of demanding power for itself; but it has also to be remembered that if it had not been for the presence of the Church mankind might well have destroyed itself completely.

On any showing Jesus was a remarkable person. As is well known, Christians insist on going much further than this in their estimate of him. They say that he is both human and divine, a real man and God at the same time. This is, on the face of it, a very queer belief, but one to which the Church has been forced by history and experience. There is no doubt that Jesus was a real man. All that we read of him in the New Testament has the unmistakable mark of genuine humanity. He was one of us – this cannot be denied. But if one tries to explain the secret of his greatness in purely human categories, the categories seem unable to stand the strain. Is it a mere man – even of the very noblest type – who entered into personal communication with his friends after his crucifixion? It may be said that the evidence for his personal resurrection (I do not here discuss whether the resurrection of which the New Testament speaks involves the emergence of his body from the tomb; let it suffice at this point that his friends were sure that it was Jesus himself, and not a ghost, to whom they were speaking and who spoke to them) is not adequate to bear the weight of such a remarkable occurrence, and that it is better to assert that the 'resurrection' was in the lives of the disciples, that is, it was an access of new life coming to them as a result of the death of Jesus. In that case we are faced with, if anything, an even more remarkable achievement on his part: the transformation by his death of a group of ordinary, disillusioned people into a revolutionary force, and the subsequent transformation of people of every sort and race and culture from then until now by the announcement of his life, teaching and death. I repeat, is this a mere man? And is it a mere man whom people today, 2,000 years after his death, claim to know personally in sacrament and prayer, and for whom men and women, under all the various tyrannies which human sinfulness and ingenuity have produced, have been prepared to die?

Jesus, then, was a man, but also more than a man. If so, he must be both human and divine. There is no middle grade between God and man into which he can be placed (except, perhaps, that of an angel, but the attempts to describe Jesus as an angel have not been very successful). The Church, recognizing this truth which is thrust upon it, has sought to define the person of Jesus in the terms of a whole succession of philosophies. Hence the doctrine of the Two Natures in Christ; hence the statement that Jesus is of 'one substance with the Father' (the English translators of the Greek words should have said 'of one *essence* with the Father', but they were misled by the Latin translation). Those who have some acquaintance with Greek thought in its pre- and post-Christian forms can understand the formulations of traditional theology to some extent. But it is doubtful whether those without the necessary training can make any sense of them at all. The striking thing is that belief in the divine humanity, or human divinity, of Christ has survived all the now discredited attempts to define it and is still as strong as ever in all Christian communities. Our own age should try, no doubt, to interpret Christ in the terms of its own philosophical approach, but it is not so likely to succeed as other ages have been, because the dominant schools of philosophy tend to rule out the very possibility of a divine humanity before it is discussed. Meanwhile, for myself I find an analogy from the arts more helpful than anything which the philosophers or psychologists offer. I think that this way of thinking about the matter came to me from Wilson Knight and Dorothy Sayers, but I do not want to ascribe to them something which they might well repudiate if they were still alive.

I put it to myself this way. An artist expresses himself through the medium he chooses, be it words, or music, or canvas and oils. If he wishes to express himself to the extent of communicating the nature of his own personality and ideals, he will write his autobiography, or produce a self-portrait, or employ his chosen medium in some other way to depict himself. The eternal Son of God, who cannot be seen or known or understood unless he communicate himself to men, chose the medium of a human life and personality for his self-portrait; and Jesus of Nazareth, fully involved in the experiences, temptations, sorrows, joys and hardships of human life, was the eternal Son of God, revealed to men.

I believe in the Holy Spirit. God is known to men as Father, Creator and Sovereign. God is known to men as Jesus, son of man and Son of God. That is, he is active in the creation and control of the world, and in the care of every human being; he is active in the disclosure of his purposes for mankind and the forgiveness of sins. He is also active in history, and in present experience, and in the worship and life of the Christian community, and in all enterprises of justice and mercy and the discovery of truth. As active in this third way, he is called God the Holy Spirit. But as the Father is distinct from the Son, so the Holy Spirit is distinct from the Son and the Father. He deals with persons as persons, and with communities as communities of persons. His greatest function is to bring the past into the present, to make the far-off events of the incarnation of Jesus Christ contemporary with us, so that we may be with him as if we were present at the Last Supper.

This lands me in the doctrine of the Holy Trinity, and I am not appalled. 'Three Persons in one God' is, of course, mathematically impossible, however much you scale down the meaning of 'person' in the phrase. Yet the experience of the Church at all times of the Father as personal, the Son as personal, and the Holy Spirit as personal, must be interpreted in such a way as to preserve the bedrock assertion that there is only one God. The personal nature of the Godhead must surely be richer and more complex than any other personal nature that we know. Is it incredible that its richness and complexity should be compatible with the co-inherence in it of three distinct personal beings? This may be a concept beyond our grasping; but should we expect anything else when we think about God?

I believe in the Holy Catholic Church, and that it exists, visible but divided, in the midst of human society. According to all the evidence we have, Christ wished his work to be continued in and by a community, not by isolated individuals, however devoted and single-minded, and the development of the Church as an institution was not contrary to his intention, though some of the forms which the institution has taken, and still more the corruptions to which it has often become prone, must surely have displeased him greatly. In spite of weakness within, and oppression from without, the Church has preserved the message transmitted to it, brought out its implications for life and thought, and applied it to the various situations of personal and corporate life; and the Gospel which it proclaims when it speaks with a united voice is recognizably the same as that with which Jesus sent out his friends to make disciples of all the nations. When a particular communion makes statements which are distinctive of itself, but not acceptable to the rest of Christendom, it is not in the same way to be trusted, for the divisions of the Church have been the most fertile source of perversions of Christian truth. Yet it has sometimes happened that one section of Christendom has re-discovered or preserved a truth which has been neglected by all other sections; and the tragedy has often been that this section, cold-shouldered by the others, has, in reaction, exalted its own particular treasure to be the sum of Christian doctrine.

The Church has an ordained ministry – with due respect to those who hold that it can and should dispense with one. An ordained minister is not of a different order of being from those who are not ordained, but, like the apostolic preachers and those who took over from them the care of the Churches, he represents the whole people of God before God and men, and at the same time represents Christ to the Church and to all mankind. But ministers do not constitute the Church; they are a small but essential part of it. They share the work that they do with those who are not ordained (though Christians disagree as to whether there is any part of the work of the Church from which laymen should be excluded), but it is proper that when the Church comes to the Holy Communion which is its central act of worship, and the act which sums up the whole Christian Gospel in word and deed, the one who celebrates it should be the one who is called and commissioned by Christ to be his ambassador and the representative of his whole people. But woe betide the Church in which the clergy reserve all the important tasks to themselves, and regard themselves as alone responsible for the care of the faithful and the impact of the Church on the world. But we live in an age in which the laypeople of Christendom have at last begun to take up their proper tasks, and perhaps no further condemnation of clericalism is necessary, even in those communions which have been particularly guilty of it in the past.

There is no evidence that Jesus established a particular form of ordained ministry, and it is notorious that, historically, the Christian ministry has developed in two main ways, the episcopal and the presbyterian, each from time to time claiming to be the one and only ministry which Christ has sanctioned. The episcopal order has the longest history, and has always been more widely spread than the other; it is very likely to be the order of the united Church of the future. But the presbyterian order may well be earlier in origin, and since its revival at the time of the Reformation has proved itself to be as worthy of its function as the episcopal order – in addition to being liable to temptations equal in strength though somewhat different in nature. There is no reason, therefore, to think that one Church order is at liberty to condemn or outlaw the other, or to suppose that the divine grace flows more freely through one than through the other.

I belong to the Methodist Church. I was not born into it, but I have grown up in it. But this is not the chief reason why I belong to it now. I owe it a great debt of gratitude, but this is not the chief reason either. I belong to it mainly because it embodies most effectively what I hold to be the most important elements in Christian faith and life. It seems to me to lay the right emphasis on the necessity for personal trust in Christ, and for steady growth in the Christian life and Christian understanding, to avoid the extremes both of sacerdotalism and individualism, and to have a truly catholic approach to doctrine, to the Church at large, and to the world outside the Church. But I could not for a moment hold that it is the only genuine form of Christianity, that Methodists have nothing to learn from other Christians, or that it is destined to be the Church of the future. On the contrary, I am aware of its many shortcomings, perhaps most of all in worship, and I am anxious for it to receive many good things from other Churches, both of the Catholic and of the Protestant tradition. Like other Churches, the Methodist Church has become excessively institutionalized, with a resultant curb on the activities of the Holy Spirit, to whom it claims to be especially devoted. It is beginning to shake itself free of this encumbrance. But the process is slow. Yet it is quite clear to me that, at least as far as my own Church is concerned, reform and renewal are carried out, under God, not by those who leave it, or leave its ministry, and criticize from outside, but by those who remain within, however uncomfortable they may sometimes become, and are willing to suffer the anguish of frustration and delay in the midst of, and for the sake of, their less forward-looking brethren.

I have given my credo. I know that there are perfectly tenable objections to everything that I have said. My cast of mind, and my training, make me constantly aware of the arguments that have been adduced against the Christian Faith. I have found the objections urged by Christians from within the Church – many of them springing from the existence of suffering, or the frequent betrayals by the Church of its own teaching – far more potent than those urged from outside. The 'outsider' rarely has a really exact idea of what he is opposing. This is, no doubt, the fault of Christians, who do not take nearly enough trouble to make themselves plain to the world at large (nor do the organs of public opinion help them to do so, for the most part); but it puts the unbeliever at a serious disadvantage. He is inclined therefore to produce an argument something of this sort: Christians believe this; but this is contrary to sound reason; therefore Christianity is untrue. But he would often find on investigation that Christians do not believe what he starts off by saying that they do believe, or that only a few of them do, or that they used to do so, but have discarded the belief.[1] Or he takes one sentence from the Christian Creed, discusses it as if it stood entirely on its own, and concludes that there is no good reason for accepting it. But the Christian Faith is a considered, unified whole, and each statement in the Creed hangs together with every other statement. The appeal of Christianity is not that it makes a number of wise statements about the world, God and man, but that it offers a coherent account of all human experience. If it is to be rebutted, it must be rebutted as a whole – it cannot be destroyed piece by piece. This, again, is no doubt irritating to the objector, but Christians cannot be expected to state their faith in the way in which their opponents would find it easiest to disprove it. Or, sometimes, the objector makes the elementary mistake of supposing that Christianity consists of a series of propositions; in fact, the heart of the matter lies elsewhere. The propositions spring from the initial encounter with God in Christ; and it would be perfectly possible for a Christian to be persuaded that all the propositions he drew from his encounter with God in Christ were unsound, and still be sure that the encounter was a genuine one. There is, perhaps, only one way in which it would be possible to disprove Christianity conclusively, and that would be by showing that there is no plan or design or pattern in any part of the universe. This has not yet been done.

But Christianity cannot be finally demonstrated either. There is, and can be, no certainty, in the proper sense of that word, about the ultimate questions of human life. Churches and Christians in the past have tried to short-circuit this problem by doctrines of the infallibility of the Church, or of the Bible, or of experience, and many Christians today would probably claim to be certain

[1] A notable example of this occurs in a recent book, *God and Philosophy*, by Antony Flew (Hutchinson, 1966). Professor Flew first defines what is meant by creation: 'God is supposed to be the Creator. This precisely means that absolutely nothing happens save by his ultimate undetermined determination and with his consenting ontological support.' Then he draws out the appalling consequences of belief in creation (pp. 43ff.). But creation does not mean to me, or, I suspect, to the great majority of Christians, anything like what Professor Flew says it does.

that their beliefs are true. But the subject matter of religious faith, which is by definition concerned with that which is beyond complete human comprehension, does not allow of certainty. We live by faith, and not by sight. A well-equipped Christian is one who has carefully scrutinized all the known ways of interpreting human life and concluded that the Christian interpretation, all things thoroughly considered, is the most satisfying to mind and heart and will (all three, of course) – or perhaps better, to the whole self – and commits himself to it.

It is common to read in obituary notices nowadays something like the following: 'Although sustained by no religious faith, Mr X devoted himself selflessly to the welfare of his fellowmen.' Clearly this fact about Mr X is to his credit – unless he gave up his religious faith for the wrong reasons. What is not to his credit is his (presumable) reasoning process. 'Although,' he seems to have argued, 'there is no God, although there is no goodness at the heart of the universe, although the universe is completely neutral, and wholly indifferent to what men call good and evil, I will nevertheless devote myself to the furtherance of good.' But what ground, in the name of logic, has he for doing so, if there is nothing in the universe, outside man, which corresponds to his concept of goodness? He might, perhaps, have answered: 'I create my own goodness, and all the other values, and then live in accordance with them.' But goodness, surely, of its very nature, if it exists at all, must be something which I recognize and accept as existing apart from me. The statement: 'I create my own values,' is very near to being a self-contradiction.

For me at least, the belief in and practice of goodness are wholly derived from my belief in God. If I ever do anything good, my motive is, firstly, gratitude to God for his love of me and of all creatures, and, secondly, the conviction that by acting well I am acting in conformity with the character of God and the nature of the universe. Therefore 'love' is a better word than 'goodness' to describe the essence of the Christian ethic. Love is of God; therefore I love God and my neighbour (when I do). Obedience to the Commandments is not the Christian ethic, though it has proved to be, and still is, a useful preparation for the Christian ethic. There is no system of laws and commands which can cover the whole variety of human situations. Moral rules are useful as *guides* to what has been proved to be right in similar cases in the past, and conscience as a useful repository of such rules. But at any moment the requirement of love may be that I break a rule in order to serve a person.

For love is a relationship between persons, and to treat other people always as persons, without coercion, flattery, or deceit, never as means to my own ends, but always as persons in their own right, as important in the scheme of things as I am myself, is almost a summary of Christian ethics. It is certainly the most important thing that Christians have to say about sex.

I believe and hope that the main pre-occupations of my professional life – teaching, preaching, writing, the whole matter of Christian Education, the renewal of worship and the reunion of the Churches – flow logically from my Christian faith. At the beginning of my career I was for twelve years Chaplain of Kingswood School, Bath, John Wesley's foundation, and I soon learned there, from the Headmaster, A. B. Sackett, and from my whole relationship with the boys in the school, that to separate the religious part of education from the rest of education makes nonsense both of education and of religion. The trouble is that this is exactly what has to be done in the vast majority of the nation's schools, because there is no agreed basis of belief among all those who teach the young or in the country as a whole. At Kingswood it was possible to give expression, not only in the chapel but in the basic principles of the school's life, to the conviction that all knowledge of man and the world in which he lives is a revelation from God, and that the meaning and purpose of all human activity is manifested in Christ; and this meant no curtailment whatever of the autonomy of individual subjects, or of the liberty of the schoolboy to opt for another faith than Christianity, or for no faith at all. This is for me the norm of what education should be. But I know very well that it cannot be carried out in most schools, though it can and should be the guiding light of a Christian who is teaching in any kind of school or college. For the rest, the important thing is that the compulsory teaching of religion – that oddity of English education of which the public still, apparently, approves – should lead to the intelligent discussion at all levels of the Christian approach to the problems of life, based on an accurate knowledge of what Christianity really teaches, and honestly compared with the other world-views which are worthy of serious consideration. The recent researches into children's appropriation of religious material which are associated with the names of Goldman and Loukes and others, have begun a new age in methods of religious teaching, and are leading to revolutionary changes which are long overdue, though the danger does exist that class room teaching may degenerate into endless discussion based on incomplete knowledge.

I suppose that, apart from my daily job, I have given more energy to the ecumenical movement than to anything else. There are obvious practical advantages in reunion; the present wastage of manpower and physical resources on the maintenance of antiquated denominational structures, in face of the steady advance of anti-Christian forces, is ludicrous and blasphemous. But my main reason for ecumenism is theological, and antedates any realization that it is a practical necessity. God is one, Christ is one, the Church is one; and any institution or practice which contradicts these truths is an anomaly which has to be abolished. Such abolition takes years of patient understanding and negotiation, for our divisions are built into our minds by our history. But the years have not been wasted, and we can now begin to see in this country and elsewhere the first signs of the harvest, in the shape of Anglican-Methodist reconciliation – which may well, if both Churches are willing, take place in 1971. And the hope kindled by the Nottingham Conference of 1964, which invited the Churches to set Easter Day, 1980, as the day of general organic reunion, has not yet been extinguished.

I intend to give the remaining years of my active life to the training of ministers for the Methodist Church, and, I hope, for the united Church of the future. The organization of all the Churches is under heavy fire from their friends, and the changes brought about by reunion are only some of the changes that will have to be carried out. The training of men for the ministry – which must soon, if Christian commonsense prevails and the confusion between tradition and prejudice is cleared up, include the training of women for the ministry also – is due for drastic reforms in the context of a changing world and a changing Church. After a slow start, these are beginning to happen. One thing, at least, is clear to me. The old method of teaching a man the Faith in great detail, and leaving him to find the way to communicate it to the people under his care, is dead. A man is not trained for the ministry unless he knows the world as well as he knows the Church, knows the Faith through and through (but not necessarily the text of the Old Testament in the original Hebrew), and is beginning to know how to communicate the Faith to the world. It is my job to help in the giving of such training. Since I believe the Christian Faith to be true, I cannot think of anything else which, for me, is more worth doing.

WILLIAM DONALD HUDSON

was born at Skipton in 1920. *He is a graduate of London University, holding degrees in Arts and Divinity and a doctorate in Philosophy. After training at Manchester Baptist College, he was ordained in* 1944 *and spent some time in the pastoral ministry. He is now Senior Lecturer in Philosophy at Exeter University. The Series,* New Studies in Ethics, *is edited by him and he is the author of* Ethical Intuitionism. *His forthcoming publications include a study of the bearing of Wittingenstein's philosophy on religious belief. He is married with three children.*

W. DONALD HUDSON

This is a personal statement, so let me begin by identifying the position from which I speak. I am a religious believer, who was born and remains within the Christian tradition; and I am also a professional philosopher who accepts for the most part contentedly, that approach to his subject generally known as linguistic analysis. I take it, then, that the question which I have to answer is: How does one manage to be both these things at the same time – a Christian theist and an analytical philosopher? This question seems to me to break down into two others: (i) what is religious belief? and (ii) can one reasonably engage in it? I do not profess to be able to answer these questions to my own entire satisfaction, let alone anyone else's. But such answers as I have I will give.

The first question – what is religious belief? – I take to call for a logical placing, for some indication of the presuppositions upon which religious belief rests and of the logical frontiers between the language in which it is expressed and other types of discourse. The second question – can one reasonably engage in it? – I shall take to expect an answer which shows whether or not there are, at least some, religious beliefs which can be held without self-contradiction or any other move which reduces them to absurdity.

What is religious belief?

It has been said that every proposition answers some question or questions; and that every question rests upon some presupposition or presuppositions.[1] This is obviously true in the case of systematic thinkers; they formulate very precisely the questions which they wish to answer, and are usually well aware of some, at least, of the presuppositions on which their questions rest.

[1] R. G. Collingwood, *An Essay on Metaphysics*, chapter iv.

The man-in-the-street may not be so conscious of the implications of what he says, but a similar analysis can be offered of the propositions which he utters. The historian – to take, at random, one instance of systematic thinking – who wrote 'Hitler's immediate reply to Mussolini had been to ask him what he needed to complete his preparations, in order to see whether Germany could supply the deficiencies',[1] was answering, amongst others, the questions 'What did Hitler do?' and 'What was his purpose in doing it?'. These questions presuppose that someone called Hitler existed and that he was capable of intentional behaviour. Equally – to take, at random, instances from conversations heard in the street – 'That's a Ford' answers 'What kind of car is that?', which presupposes that there are cars of different kinds; and 'That's a bad thing for him to have done' answers 'What was the moral value of his action?', which presupposes that an action has been done and that it is possible to evaluate such actions morally. The presuppositions, whether of the systematic thinker or the man-in-the-street, in these simple illustrations, are, of course, themselves propositions open to question: it would make perfectly good sense to ask 'Did Hitler exist?' or 'Are there different kinds of car?', though no one would be in any doubt about the answers.

But the point which I wish to make now is that there are presuppositions of discourse which are ultimate in the sense that they are not open to question as those which we have just considered are.

Let me give some examples. A physical scientist, as such, presupposes that there are physical objects. However minute or fleeting his particles, that is what they are. If he talks at all, he talks about physical objects. So 'There are physical objects' is not for him a proposition which may be true or false, which may have scientific evidence for, or against, it. It is the ultimate presupposition of his whole universe of discourse.

Similarly the historian (and here I differentiate him very carefully from the social scientist) presupposes free agency; that is, beings who are capable of forming intentions or making choices and acting accordingly. The historian, as such, explains what goes

[1] A. Bullock, *Hitler*, p. 494.

on, not by reference to causal laws linking physical bodies or spatio-temporal events, but to principles of action which he and his readers consider reasonable. He makes intelligible to us what some personage has done by so describing the circumstances of the action that we 'see the point' of it, we understand what the agent was 'up to'. And we do this when we are shown that his action was in accordance with what we should consider 'the thing to do' in such circumstances. Of course, there is a difference between understanding and approving; and I do not necessarily mean that what the agent does has our commendation. What I do mean is that we can see a *reason* for it. To recall the quotation of a moment ago for example, if we asked 'Why did Hitler so reply to Mussolini?', the answer 'Mussolini was his ally' would make sense of what Hitler did, because we consider it reasonable to assist one's allies; but if the reply were 'Mussolini was a fat man', it would not, because we do not consider it reasonable to assist a man simply if he is fat. My point here is that the whole structure of historical explanation is geared to free agency; its subject matter is what is taken to be free, intentional behaviour, and essential to its methodology is the concept of a reasonable principle of action. 'Is there free agency?', then, is not an open question for the historian; it is the presupposition of his whole discipline.[1]

The moralist, to take a third example, cannot, as such, answer the question 'Is there moral value?', for his whole way of thinking presupposes that there is. The concept of moral value is logically irreducible; as so many philosophers have pointed out, to say that X is good, right or obligatory, in the moral sense, is not logically equivalent to saying that X maximises happiness, conduces to evolution, fulfills the will of God, or to describing it in any other such naturalistic, or supernaturalistic, terms. It is to say something which is *sui generis*. If the moralist, *qua* moralist, talks at all, he does so in terms of moral value.[2]

What I have been endeavouring to show, then, is that there are these various universes of discourse, which have, respectively, their own definitive presuppositions or constitutive concepts. What I now claim is that religious belief is similar in this respect.

[1] Cf. W. H. Dray, *Laws and Explanation in History*.
[2] Cf. my *Ethical Intuitionism* (New Studies in Ethics).

Its definitive presupposition is the concept of divine agency (or agencies). To make it clear that I do not simply have theism in mind when I speak of this concept, I will call it the concept of god (with a small 'g'). When I am thinking of the particular content which Christian theists give to it, I shall speak of God (with a capital 'G'). The kind of question which the religious believer, as such, answers is 'What is god doing?', 'What is god's will?', etc.: and the presupposition of such questions – that there is god – is ultimate.

Let me digress for a moment to acknowledge two things. In effect, I am excluding from the application of the word 'religion' any system of belief or practice which dispenses with the concept of divine agency altogether, and I recognize that this may be contrary to ordinary usage (e.g. some forms of Buddhism). Nevertheless, whatever we call it, there is, I maintain, a universe of discourse constituted by the concept of god and that is what I am talking about when I say religious belief. Then again, I acknowledge that there are 'gods many and lords many'. The nature and, so to say, content of 'god' is a matter for discussion within religion, just as the nature and content of the physical world is in natural science, or of agency, in history, or of duty, in morals. As a Christian believer, of course, I would wish to participate in such a discussion; but whether or not the Christian concept of god is preferable to any other is beside the point at present. The first essential is to give religious belief its correct logical placing. Disputes *within* it are religious or theological, rather than philosophical, and I am not writing about these here.

I must now try to make clearer what I mean by saying that the concept of god is constitutive of a universe of discourse. I mean at least three things.

One is that this concept constitutes religious belief in the sense that it is the believer's guiding principle. It guides him in the way, for example, that the principle, every event has a cause (or can be related in terms of some universal law with other events), guides the scientist. If the latter comes upon some event which he cannot thus fit into his scheme, he does not conclude that it can never be so fitted; he concludes that he has either failed to observe some relevant feature of it, or needs to formulate his laws more carefully in order to provide for it. *Qua* scientist, he never doubts that what goes on in the world can be brought under universal laws connecting spatio-temporal events. Well, somewhat similarly, I am saying, the religious believer never doubts that what goes on in the world can be brought under the concept of divine agency. If he comes upon some event for which he cannot immediately provide a rationale in these terms – concerning which, for instance, he cannot answer the question 'What is god doing here?' – he does not conclude that there is no such rationale. He sets himself to think more carefully about the event or god – or both – until he finds one. Any theistic discussion of what is called the problem of evil would provide a paradigm case of such exertions.[1]

A second, and related, sense in which the concept of god is constitutive of religious belief is this: it determines what, for the believer, counts as an explanation and what does not. It has been said that he 'has a blik', 'adopts an onlook', 'uses a picture'.[2] However expressed, the point is that he is committed to a concept or set of concepts which determines what is intelligible to him and what is not. This is just another way of saying that the blik (etc.) is presupposed in the questions he asks and so necessarily in any answers to them. He is not, of course, alone in having *a* blik, onlook or picture; what is distinctive about him is *the* one which he has. The scientist asks 'What things are there in the world and how are they related?', the historian, 'What have men done?', the moralist, 'What has moral value?' – and the religious believer, 'What is god up to?' His blik, onlook or picture, when he says precisely what he means by it, may be very complicated, and his answers to questions based upon it even more so. It constitutes what he means by god. It also constitutes what is for him an explanation and what is not.

Thirdly, the concept of god is constitutive of religious belief because it gives a certain character to the believer's experience, or part of it. It is a mistake to suppose that our experiences just come to us, so to say, conceptually raw. To experience X is to ex-

---

[1] E.g. my 'An Attempt to Defend Theism', *Philosophy*, 1964.

[2] Cf. R. M. Hare, 'Theology and Falsification' in *New Essays in Philosophical Theology*, edited by Flew and MacIntyre; D. D. Evans, *The Logic of Self-Involvement;* L. Wittgenstein, *Lectures and Conversations.*

perience it *as* X; and to experience it as X is to take it to be an instance of what is *called* X. The character of our experience, therefore, is to some degree at least, contingent upon the conceptual scheme within which are conscious of it. Take, as an example, remorse. Would it be possible for anyone who did not deal in the questions and answers of morality to feel remorse? Surely not! Similarly, it seems to me quite clear that there are kinds of experience peculiar to those who deal in the questions and answers of religion. To have one's heart strangely warmed, as Wesley says that he did, is not to suffer from heartburn. It is to have a peculiar kind of experience, built into which there is some thought of god. How our experience comes to have the character which it has is, no doubt, a much more complicated matter than I have made it appear; but that this character is, to some extent, constituted by the conceptual scheme within which we are aware of it seems to me indisputable. Religious experiences do not occur to those who have no concept of god.

What I have been arguing, then, is, first, that the logical analysis of religious belief shows it to have the same *general* features as any other universe of discourse. But, secondly, it differs from all others in the *particular* that its constitutive concept is that of god. We are now, I think, in a position to see precisely where the problem about the rationality of religious belief, if there is one, must be located. It is in this concept. The relevant questions are: Is the concept of god internally coherent and consistent? What would determine the reasonableness or otherwise of thinking in terms of it? And, when that is clear, is it reasonable to do so or not? To these questions I must turn in a moment. There is, however, one final point of some importance to be made about what religious belief is.

The reader may feel, in the light of what he has read here so far, that all one can really say is that a religious believer is a person who is committed irrevocably to the belief that god exists. But this is certainly not all that one can say; and perhaps it is not what one is saying at all. A man could believe that god exists much as he could believe that the Loch Ness monster or Venusians exist. But would that make him a religious believer? No: religious belief is certainly more than, and perhaps quite other than, assent to the proposition that a being (or beings), god, exists. A man could assent to 'god exists', as to 'The Loch Ness monster exists' or 'Venusians exist', without it making a scrap of difference to the way he thinks or acts in any other respect; but that would assuredly not be religious belief, as usually understood. At the very least, we must say that the belief that god exists is not a sufficient condition of religious belief.

Is it a necessary condition? One philosopher[1] has recently contended that a person in what he calls the faith attitude – as we should say, a religious believer – would never say that he believed *that* God loves him. Rather would he say, or intend to say, that he *felt* God's love for him. I think one could extend the point and hold that neither would he say, or intend to say, that he believed *that* god exists, but rather that he felt (in a sense to be read off from the three points which I made in defining what it means to say that god is the constitutive concept of a universe of discourse) god's existence. As the philosopher referred to remarks, 'beliefs *that*' are, no doubt, the precursors and consequences of the faith attitude; but they must not be confused with it.

Remarkable as it may seem, it is therefore quite mistaken to say that the difference between religious believers and unbelievers is that the former belief that god exists and the latter that he does not. As Wittgenstein showed in his recently published lectures on religious belief, the difference is more complicated than, and indeed not at all like, this. It is that the believer has a 'picture' and 'uses' it in accordance with a 'technique', whereas the unbeliever does not have the picture, or at least does not so use it. The believer makes the picture 'guidance for this life. . . . Whenever he does anything, this is before his mind . . . he has what you might call an unshakeable belief. It will show . . . by regulating for in all his life.'[1]

Can one reasonably engage in religious belief?

'Reasonable' and 'unreasonable' are evaluative terms; but it is

---

[1] H. H. Price, 'Faith and Belief' in *Faith and the Philosophers*, edited by J. Hick; cf. also his 'Belief "In" and Belief "That" ' *Religious Studies*, 1965.

[2] *Lectures and Conversations*, pp. 53–54. Cf. my forthcoming small book, *Ludwig Wittgenstein: The Bearing of his Philosophy upon Religious Belief*.

not always easy to define the criteria in accordance with which they are being, or should be, used. We must consider what these words mean with reference to religious belief.

To begin with, if such belief is to be reasonable, then what is said about the concept of god, which constitutes it, must not be self-contradictory.

Some of the statements which some of my fellow-theists, for instance, make about God seem to me to be plainly self-contradictory. To take one example, consider Rudolf Otto's words: 'Not the most concentrated attention can elucidate the object to which this (*sc.* numinous) state of mind refers, bringing it out of the impenetrable obscurity of feeling into the domain of the conceptual understanding.'[1] The author clearly intends his 'can' to be logical; but if it is not, as he implies, logically possible to know what the 'object' (i.e. god) is, how logically can we know that it is to this object that the state of mind 'refers'? Or, to take another example, theists sometimes say that words like 'good' or 'loving' have a meaning when applied to God, different from that which they have when used of men. Fair enough, provided that some account, which does not contradict itself, is given of this difference. But we are sometimes told that sense can be made of the statement that God is good or loving – even though what he is said to have done, if done by a man, would imply that he is neither – simply by introducing the qualification 'infinitely' before 'good' and 'loving' (and thus the problem of evil is solved!). What is being claimed for 'infinitely' here, if not that it licenses us to say 'good' when we mean 'not good'?

The trouble with contradictions, such as these, is that from them anything can be shown to follow. It makes no difference that they are about god. To utter a contradiction – to say that you know god who is unknowable, or that god is good in the sense of both good and bad – is tantamount to saying nothing at all. Since anything follows from a contradiction, it is no more significant than if you had said nothing at all. I contend that it is not necessary to say such things in order to be a Christian theist. When I say that I believe that God has revealed himself in Christ, I feel no necessity to add that I do not know who he is; and when I say

---

[1] *The Idea of the Holy* (Pelican edition), p. 74.

that I believe him to be transcendantally good, I mean that his goodness is very, very great, greater than any we have witnessed elsewhere, perhaps greater than we can imagine, but I certainly do not mean that in his case 'goodness' includes 'badness' (though I concede that this leaves me with the problem of evil still on my hands!).[1] Whatever may be said against these beliefs of mine, they are not self-contradictory; and I would claim that they represent the beliefs of most Christian theists who have not been corrupted by bad philosophy.

There is, however, a more vexing problem. Some would say that the concept of god, at least as Christians define it, is inherently self-contradictory. They point out that Christians believe, on the one hand, that God acts in the world; and on the other, that he is not a spatio-temporal object, does not, that is, have a physical body. They add that it does not make sense thus to speak of acting without a body. Doesn't it? The problem is complicated and I have written more fully about it elsewhere.[2] Here I must content myself with making one or two points summarily. The essential one, I think, is that agency is logically distinct from bodily movement, and this not only in the case of god but in every case. A human agent is always other than his 'situation', as it has been called; and part of his situation is his physical body, so he is always logically distinct from that. The distinction may be seen in these ways. You can as intelligibly ask an agent what he is going to do about the fact that he has lost a limb or lost his memory as about the fact that he has lost his money. His body – limbs and memory – is not logically different in this regard from the rest of his situation – his money etc. Moreover, what is happening on any occasion in terms of agency can (logically) never be reduced to an account of what is going on in terms of causally connected spatio-temporal events; for whatever account of this latter kind is given, it still makes sense to ask 'But what was the agent doing?' This question has point because the same account in terms of bodily movement will invariably accord with different answers to it. For instance, the same account of bodily movements might accord with these answers to 'What was he doing?':

[1] Cf. my 'An Attempt to Defend Theism', op.cit., for how I would deal with it.
[2] Cf. my article on 'Transcendence', *Theology*, 1966.

'Trying to win the Grand Prix', 'Trying to commit suicide', 'Trying to murder his rival', etc. I concede two things: (i) that it does not make sense to speak of agency where nothing describable in terms of spatio-temporal events occurs, and (ii) that bodily movement is essential to the concept of a person, though not to that of an agent. Two consequences follow from these concessions: (i) I cannot say that God has acted in the world where no spatio-temporal events have occurred; (ii) I cannot say that God is a person. But I have no desire to say either of these things. I never claim that God has acted where nothing describable in terms of spatio-temporal event has occurred. Nor do I claim that he is a person, except figuratively. What I do claim is that since, even in the case of human agency, there is no logically essential difference between the agent's body and the rest of his physical situation, i.e. as agent he is distinct from both, it is perfectly intelligible to speak of an agency, such as God's, which undoubtedly has its situation, but nothing within that situation, distinct from all the rest, which is referred to as God's body. It may, of course, be said that this whole language of agency, whether used of god or man, is superstitious and should be dropped. But when one considers what would have to go with it – all religion, all morality, all history, most literature and much art – I find the proposal ridiculous. It is tantamount to proposing that we should stop talking as, to and about human beings. But, this apart, I shall be content if I have shown that divine agency is no more unintelligible than human. In neither case can acting, as such, be reduced to bodily movement. It is therefore no more nonsensical to speak of god acting well or lovingly than of man doing so.

I conclude, then, that it is possible to have a concept of god which is not self-contradictory. But unfortunately for those who wish to believe as I do, even if this is so, it does not appear to follow that, in every sense of the word, it is reasonable to be a religious believer. There are, some would say, at least two further necessary conditions of reasonableness.

(i) One is that the believer must have good grounds for believing that god exists. Admittedly, this may not be a sufficient condition of a religious belief, as we have seen, but we cannot get away with denying that it is a necessary one. It is all very well to say that such belief is constituted by the concept of god; but there is an endless number of concepts, each of which could constitute a universe of discourse. Surely the reasonable man, as such, must have some criterion for determining which of these he will engage in and which not; and what can it be except the criterion, 'Does the constitutive concept of this universe of discourse refer to what really exists or not?' I agree that he must have some criterion, but I do not think that this can be it. Consider what would be involved in any answer, which you gave, to the question, 'Does god really exist or not?' There are only two alternatives.

First, that you should *assume* that the constitutive concept of one universe of discourse refers to what really exists and then, in effect, ask: Is god that? Now, if the concept, which you assume, is that of god, your question will be loaded in such a way that the answer is necessarily yes; but if your concept is anything else, it will be so loaded that the answer is necessarily no. The view, which Bertrand Russell says he early took and has retained, that no theological proposition should be accepted unless there is the same kind of evidence for it that would be required for a proposition in science, seems to me to be an instance of this latter loading.[1] What Russell is, in effect, insisting we should ask is: Is god a physical object?

But now the second alternative. If you claim to have answered the question: Does god really exist? without assumptions which beg it one way or another, then you are claiming, in effect, to have got 'outside' all conceptual schemes whatever and come to know which of their several constitutive concepts fit real existence and which do not. But how logically can you know anything outside all conceptual schemes? You must conceive of it in order to know it.

To answer the question: Does god really exist?, in accordance with the first alternative, requires you to beg it; in accordance with the second, to do what is logically impossible. It is not a necessary condition of reasonableness in religious believers or anyone else to do either of these things. Indeed, it is definitive of reasonableness not to! I conclude therefore that one can reasonably engage in religious belief without showing that god really exists.

[1] B. Russell, *Autobiography*, vol. i. p. 41.

(ii) Another necessary condition of reasonableness, so some say, is scepticism.[1] The reasonable man is definitively the man who holds *all* his beliefs provisionally. He is always accessible to considerations which may require him to change or modify them. He is irrevocably committed to nothing. The problem is: Can a religious believer, as such, fulfil this condition? Is it not only psychologically difficult for him but also logically impossible?

Let us concede the psychological difficulty. Religious believers do not readily give up their cherished beliefs. But then neither, so far as I can see, do, for example, politicians or moralists; and even scientists seem frequently to be more reluctant to change their minds than one might have expected. I am not convinced that it is necessarily a more traumatic experience to surrender a belief about god than it is to cross the floor of the House or see a theory, on the strength of which you hoped to be elected to the Royal Society, disproved.

The important point, however, is whether or not it is logically impossible for a religious believer to be as sceptical as, on the view which we are considering, a thinker needs to be in order to be rational. One's first inclination is to reply that the limits of scepticism in the case of religion are no different from those in any other universe of discourse. After all, it is logically impossible for a physical scientist to remain such, if he stops believing in the physical world; or a historian, if he dispenses with the concept of agency; or a moralist, if he comes to the conclusion that it makes no sense to talk about moral value. May we not say that it is only in a way similar to each of these that the religious believer is irrevocably committed: i.e. it is logically impossible for him to be a religious believer, if he surrenders his belief in god?

I doubt if we can simply leave it at that. There is, or seems to be, an important difference between religious belief and other universes of discourse. *Within* the others, it is generally recognized that, under certain conditions, one must be willing to modify, or abandon, a belief; and this willingness is taken to be a defining characteristic of the reasonable man. True, scientists or historians, for instance, may in practice be unwilling to give up their theories but they do not make a virtue of such unwillingness as re-

[1] Cf. W. W. Bartley, *The Retreat to Commitment.*

ligious believers appear to do. The religious believer with un-shakeable convictions tends to be admired, by his fellow believers, and nowadays not only by those who share his convictions but also by those who do not. 'We respect each other's opinions' is widely said in religion. But, in other spheres, it is not the mark of the reasonable man that he admires convictions for being unshakeable, but for being correct; and, where there are differences of opinion, it is characteristic of him, not that he respects them all, but that he knows how to resolve them.

The trouble in religion is that there seem to be no generally agreed methods of determining who is speaking the truth and who is not. Various such methods have been proposed: the appeal to scripture or tradition within a religion, the appeal to experience or moral consequences, as between one religion and another, etc. But such criteria, even if not inherently unsatisfac-tory, tend to be indefinable in precise terms so that one can always introduce a saving hypothesis to protect oneself against defeat by an opponent. This is why, even within such a restricted area as that of the Ecumenical Movement within Christianity, re-ligious believers seem able to talk endlessly about their differ-ences, to concede every point made against each other, and yet to resolve nothing.

These two features – the apparent respect for conviction *per se* and the apparent lack of any clearly stateable and generally recognized criteria for settling differences – must give pause to anyone who wishes to say that it is reasonable to engage in re-ligious belief. But is the position hopeless? The notion of ration-ality which we are considering here may, of course, be wrong, but what if it is not? May one suggest that, then, there is a great task of analysis, which philosophers of religion need to under-take? It will cover the whole field of religious belief; it will extract certain common features of the concept of god in differing re-ligions; in the light of these and with reference, of course, to the lines of development in experience and doctrine, which can be matched between one religion and another, it will enunciate criteria for determining what is true or false where god is con-cerned, which will have some hope of being accepted by educated and intelligent men in each religious tradition. Thus a framework will be provided comparable to those within which scientists, historians or moralists, respectively, work. Two consequences at least will follow. One: it will then be possible to be reasonable in religion in the sense in which it is possible to be so in other spheres. It will be possible, that is, to be a 'religious sceptic': to hold one's beliefs open to change within their universe of discourse. Thus to hold beliefs provisionally is not to be uncommitted or dispassionate – the reasonable scientist commits himself to a theory every time he goes to work, and the reasonable moralist may back his judgment with his life. My religious sceptic would not be in any sense an unbeliever. He could hold what he believes about god provisionally and yet stake all upon it. The other consequence, if such a framework as I suggest could be provided, is this: the frontiers of the experience within which it is possible for the believer to participate, will be enlarged. As discussion and understanding across erstwhile impassable frontiers becomes possible and is given some point, the 'form of life', to use a term of Wittgenstein's, which religious belief constitutes, will be, for any given believer, extended. It will then make sense to speak of religious conviction, not as the defence of a position in dogma, but as the exploration of a dimension of experience, the dimension of god.

I cannot see anything false to Christian theism in these remarks. If Christ was who he said he was, then what I am advocating will constitute a mapping of the road that leads to him, or at least of the country within which he may be discovered. But it may well involve the bypassing of many things which have been said about him.

Conclusion

I have tried, then, to set out my answer to the two questions which are inescapable for one who is both a Christian and a philosopher. It may be objected that all I have shown, if I have shown anything, is that there is not good reason to *give up* religious belief, if one has it; but that I have failed to provide any good reason why one should *adopt* it, if one does not have it. In reply, I can only say two things. First, that this is a personal statement and necessarily reflects how the questions have come to me. I do not know what it is like not to have any religious beliefs and to be looking for a good reason why one should adopt some. But I do know what it is like to believe in God and find that belief called in question. Secondly, I have no clear conception of what conditions an argument would have to fulfil in order to provide a good reason why one should be a religious believer. Presumably this is what is meant by saying that faith is a gift of God. That remark does not seem to me absurd. The request 'Give me a reason for believing in god' strikes me as not unlike 'Give me one for believing in physical objects, or agency or moral value'. The request looks so plausible, but can it be met in these latter cases any more than in the former? It does not for a moment follow, if the second request cannot be met, that reasonable men must therefore have nothing to do with science, history or morality. Nor does it follow, if this request cannot be met in god's case that they must give up religion.

All you can do, in the last analysis, is give, not so much a reason as an invitation. It is the invitation to explore what Wittgenstein might have called a 'proto-phenomenon', a 'language game', a 'form of life',[1] to ask a certain kind of question and to put yourself in the way of a certain kind of experience, confident at least that there are no good reasons why you shouldn't. It is the invitation which the Founder of Christianity expressed thus: 'Come and see.'[2]

---

[1] See his *Philosophical Investigations*, 654 and p. 226.
[2] *St John*, i. 39.

JOHN LAWRENCE

was born in 1907. *He received a classical education at Eton and New College, Oxford, and qualified as a solicitor. He is married, with no children. He speaks and reads Russian, French and Italian fluently, and German and Spanish less fluently.*

In 1939 *he worked with the German Jewish Aid Committee, and then joined the B.B.C., where he became European Service Organizer. In* 1942 *he left the B.B.C. to become the first British Press Attaché in the U.S.S.R., where he remained till* 1945, *when he was awarded the O.B.E. In Russia he founded the* British Ally, *an uncensored weekly newspaper in Russian which circulated throughout the Soviet Union. He is now editor of* Frontier, *a lay, international, ecumenical quarterly, which circulates in all countries and among the leaders of all Churches. His book,* A History of Russia, *has been through several editions and is available as a paperback in Mentor Books.*

JOHN LAWRENCE

'The God Who Shows Himself
And The God Who Hides Himself'

The content of my belief is not fixed at any moment. It changes and grows, like a shoot on the vine outside my window. For twenty years now the growth has had an organic continuity and consistency, but it is only by degrees that I am coming to see the fuller implications of what I believe. So I must begin by describing the process by which I came to believe anything at all, and I must give some account of things which are only now entering my consciousness.

I cannot remember a time when I did not know what it was to feel the glory of God, to be sensible of his law filling the world. The origin of these feelings goes back behind my conscious memories, but I think I was initiated into these mysteries by a governess who came for a short time when I was very young. Naturally, at this early age my religious consciousness was supported by no framework of ordered thought, and, as I grew up, I made no attempt to put my ideas in order. Ours was a religious household, but it was assumed that theology was nonsense and I remember looking with amazement at editions of the early fathers in other peoples' libraries. Such things were not for us and their utility, if any, was long ago exhausted.

I received two things from this background; the memory of a vision that could never be effaced, and a confusion of ideas, which made it hard to relate my religion to the rest of my experience, and which in the end destroyed all belief. I was confirmed, but no one attempted to explain the Creed to me. So I had no clear idea why I was being confirmed, beyond that I was expressing a belief in God as father and a rather vague loyalty to Christ. Yet, if I had no theology, I had certain presuppositions. First, that Christians could expect no monopoly of truth and, second, that this age

113

was no wiser than other ages. So I was ready to find truth expressed at other times and in other places as much as in my own time and country.

I tried Hinduism but could not make head or tail of it. With the Chinese poets, philosophers and artists I felt at home. Their rhythm and their concrete, earthy ways of perception were congenial. Though it is many years since I soaked myself in the civilization of the far east, the influence has persisted. From the Confucians I leant respect for other peoples' feelings, for order and the way things ought to be, but I learnt still more from the Taoists. The universe has a grain and one must cut according to the grain. This is the Tao, 'the way of heaven and earth'. Do things according to the Way and they will go easily. Go against the Way and you come to a stop. I would almost say that things are either easy or impossible, but never difficult. If writing this essay suddenly becomes difficult, I shall suspect that I am going against the Tao. What I am able to understand of Taoism seems to me entirely consonant with Christianity, and is, indeed, a beautiful commentary on the doctrine of 'works' and 'grace'. It is not possible to get right with the world, with oneself or with God by making special efforts. The Way must be shown by grace and then no effort seems hard. From the Taoists, too, I learnt to be suspicious of cleverness, sharp thoughts, and intellectual haste.

At Oxford I read Greats and my attitude to belief was shaped for ever. I had no gift for philosophy, but this helped, in a way, to show me the limits of human reason. Tutorials with the stern Horace Joseph left me out of breath and humiliated. H. A. Pritchard's lectures on the Theory of Knowledge showed me once and for all that the systematic arguments of the greatest minds have fatal flaws. H. H. Price's lectures on the Theory of Perception showed the incredible treachery of appearances. I concluded that no human knowledge has a basis in proof, but I did not conclude that we have no knowledge. A thing may be true, even if you cannot prove it.

The difficulty seemed to be that no single thing was fully intelligible unless you could grasp its relation to every other thing throughout the universe. But the universe is infinite and our minds are finite. So it did not surprise me much that the search for a water-tight theory of knowledge ended in an *impasse*. The world being like this, the problem of knowledge became a problem of action. How was one to behave in a world where nothing could be proved?

I still wanted to see how things connected, for it seemed, or I assumed, that the universe must have some ultimate coherence. My reading was desultory but my interest was almost universal. History and pre-history reached out into palaeontology. I read some books about astronomy and physics, and there were even fleeting moments when I thought I was beginning to understand relativity. But my lack of mathematics soon closed that road. In all this it never occurred to me to consider the possibility of revelation, the possibility that, if the world had a purpose, some clues to that purpose might have been deliberately put in our hands.

This being so, the vague but vivid beliefs with which I started were slowly worn away over more than twenty years. I went to church less and less often, and I should have found it hard to say why I did so at all. I never said my prayers. Perhaps I should have settled for the grey world that was slowly opened before me, if I could have forgotten my childhood's vision of splendour. But when the last glow had faded from the horizon the world seemed by contrast inexpressibly cold and dreary. I was acutely unhappy for a short time. Then I considered the fact that if nothing was proved, equally nothing was disproved. I noticed that all that I felt had been felt with great intensity by some of the early Victorians, such as Tennyson and Clough. Ought I not to look again at Christian belief? So I got out my Greek Testament and began to read St Mark's Gospel, a few verses every day. When I was about half way through I began to ask myself 'who, then, was Jesus?' Was he more than a man? After that I was over the top of the hill.

Soon there came crowding in on me all the questions which perplexed the early Church. If Jesus was more than a man, in what sense was he a man? If he was God, what is his relation to the Father? Surely there can't be two Gods? The idea of the Son as a slightly subordinate God, which was held by Arius, was even less convincing. And so on. The answers given to such questions by the despised early fathers were illuminating and cogent, now that I had come to stand where they stood. Their answers had been summarized in the Creeds which now cast a bright light into some very dark corners.

I believe every word of the Apostles' Creed and the Nicene Creed. But they are still human words and therefore insufficient to describe the realities of which they speak. They give us pointers to ultimate things which, in this life, we can only touch with the tips of our fingers. God does indeed show himself in Jesus, through the Holy Spirit, and indeed in the whole process of revelation to which the Bible witnesses. But he hides himself too (Isaiah 45 : 15). We should never know him at all if he did not show himself, but we should never grow up if he did not also hide himself sometimes. How are we to understand this paradox?

'No man has at any time seen God', says the New Testament, while the Old Testament assumes that anyone who did see God would be killed by the splendours of the sight. Surely this is right, both ways. We cannot see God because we have not the faculties to do so and if *per impossible* we did see him, we should be destroyed by the sight. In heaven we shall see him, and we shall be strengthened to do so. That is what heaven is for. On earth we have to be left in the dark about many things that we should like to know, because our eyes cannot yet stand much light. If we were now told the answer to some of our riddles, such as free will, we should not understand. Indeed we should probably not even see that it was an answer. Yet there is progress towards understanding and towards seeing. If God is unknowable to us in his inner being, he makes himself known to us through what he does, and the strange thing is that this knowledge of God is not an indirect, inferential knowledge but a direct knowledge, as direct as one's knowledge of one's own self. This perception of God comes at totally unpredictable moments in prayer, and particularly through the sacraments, but it comes through action, too, which is the core of truth in that rather misleading adage, *laborare est orare* (to work is to pray).

God's mode of showing himself to us has two peculiarities. It is embodied in particularities and it is expressed in symbols. We may wish it were otherwise but we have to accept it as it is. Generalizations, such as I am now tempted to make, are not God's way. He shows himself to us in the form of a man, a village carpenter. He shows his will for mankind by choosing an individual, Abraham, and then one of his descendants, Jacob, and by helping the race descended from them to draw their conclusions about his wider purpose for humanity. The Bible is the record we have been given of God's showing of himself to us. Sometimes it gives us precise concrete detail about the actions of particular people such as David or Pontius Pilate, but a large part of both the Old and New Testaments is poetry and the Bible speaks characteristically through symbols and images.

There is no certain way of telling when the Bible is giving one facts, and when it is giving one a poetical description of something because that is the best way to tell the truth about it, or when it is just being inaccurate. But none of this worries me much. It does not matter that the formula for pi is given wrongly in II Kings 7:23 or that the Old Testament is as unreliable about figures as other ancient writers. That is not what the Bible is for. Parts of Genesis are plainly poetical and other parts are proto-history. Job and Jonah are invented stories. The carrying away of Israel into captivity is a historical fact, as is the trial and passion of Our Lord. It does not disturb me that there are many passages where one cannot tell just how much is fact and how much is interpretation. I believe in the empty tomb not for the Biblical evidence alone, strong though that is, but because the total record of the Bible and its working out in the life of the Church have convinced me that Jesus lives and that he was God incarnate. It is possible to construct theories of the Resurrection which deny that Jesus rose bodily from the dead, but I find them over-elaborate and unconvincing, and I do not see how to square them with the Bible's emphasis on bodily things in general and the bodily resurrection in particular. If the record is wrong on that point, I see no sufficient reason to believe in any other view of the Resurrection. The Incarnation is the central miracle, if miracle be the word, and everything else follows from that.

I am prepared to study such questions with an interest that is mixed with scepticism about the conclusions of scholars on a matter where the evidence is so unusual. But when I read the Bible every morning I pay little attention to learned theories. I try to give myself entirely to the immediate impact of what I am reading. 'Except ye become as little children . . .' Whatever the events may have been, I know that this is the record of them that God means me to have. If I miss reading the Bible any day, it is as if my food had been without salt. In recent years I have read the Old Testament more than the New. This is partly because my knowledge of the Old Testament needed badly to be strengthened, and partly because the current tendency to give one a wholly New Testament religion results in a shallow and sentimental Christianity. The Old Testament is indeed dangerous to morality, if you regard it as primarily a collection of moral tales, but that is not what it is. I read it as the record of the way in which God led his people through very tough circumstances and of the groping and unwilling way in which they gradually began to perceive what he required of them. It reminds me of the song 'You never notice how I love you'. The toughness and realism of the Old Testament makes it particularly opposite to what is happening in many countries in the second half of this century. And God's ways with his ancient people the Jews help one to understand what he is doing today with his Church, the New Israel. I find that the Old Testament renews my courage in a special way, so that I can face the sometimes daunting circumstances of God's people today.

It is the truth that matters. And truth is not changed by our shifting opinions. Truth is unchanging but our apprehension of it is a process of unfolding. Therefore one must be open to every question that is asked. This is not to say that 'yes' is the answer to every question, but no conclusion must be taken for granted. This is not easy, for everyone has doubts, and the simplest way, if not the most efficacious way, of dealing with doubts is to bottle them up. There are moments when one wonders whether the Holy Communion is anything more than an European counterpart of the Japanese tea ceremony. In prayer one may feel like a man who picks up a telephone that has been disconnected. Or perhaps it has never been connected? My experience is that such questions fade away and become irrelevant if one takes them calmly, and gives one's mind time to sort them out, and then turns to God.

Similarly, in spite of much that is said, I do not think the Creeds are outdated or that the images used in Scripture have lost their relevance. I am not even sure that the difficulty of conveying their truth to modern man is greater than it has always been; it was never easy. If we fail more nowadays, it may be because we assume that we *shall* fail. Sometimes I detect signs of panic in myself, when some belief that I hold dear seems threatened. At such times the words spoken to Joshua often come into my mind spontaneously, 'Only be thou strong and very courageous'. This puts heart into me and I find it easier to listen without getting rattled.

I could not believe a Christianity which seemed discontinuous with its own past. If there is a special kind of truth for this generation, it is certain to be rejected by the next generation. If I, or anyone, seek truth at all, we seek a truth that is universal, that is true everywhere, that has always been true and always will be true, 'that which was from the beginning'. Yet unchanging truth may require a new expression in each age. God is 'out there', because he is everywhere, but for the same reason he is also found dwelling in our hearts and can be spoken of as 'the ground of our being'. I think of God as being above all 'the God within', but I know that none of these ways of speaking limits him. He escapes whatever words I use, so that it is very hard to say anything at all about him. Our words are not made for that purpose. I like the Hindu story of the sage who was asked three times by his pupil 'What is Brahman (the ground of being)?' After remaining silent twice, he replied the third time 'Brahman is silence'. If he had been aware of Christianity, he might have gone on to say 'Brahman is the Word'. The eternal Word of God is utterly different from human words; in one sense the Word is silence, but it is a silence that is filled with life and meaning.

I should like to accept the traditional formulation of the universality of Christian truth in the aphorism *quod semper, quod ubique, quod ab omnibus creditum est* (what has always been believed, everywhere and by all). But this phrase conceals the assumption that the substance of Christianity can properly be expressed in a series of propositions, which is at best a half truth. Moreover it is impossible to find an adequate series of propositions which have always been believed by all Christians everywhere. Yet the Christian community has been led by the Holy Spirit through the ages. I believe accordingly that there is a core of truth in everything that has been believed by very large numbers of Christians for a long time. I do not believe some of the terrible things that have been taught about hell and purgatory at various times and places, but I cannot doubt that there is judgment and that it is a fearful thing to answer for what I am and what I have done. I believe that there is a fundamental unity of Christian experience which must be sought continually.

But the search goes even wider than that. The relation between Christianity and other religions is extremely subtle and the real encounter between the religions of the world is only now beginning. The Christian revelation is in itself complete; yet our grasp of it is imperfect. In consequence I am already finding that my understanding of my own religion is being changed by contact with other faiths. Hindus and Buddhists deny final value to personality, whereas we affirm it, but is what they deny the same as what we affirm? This question has brought me to reconsider what I mean by personality; and in doing so I have been helped both by modern psychology and by the Christian tradition. There is a tradition running from the Gospels (Mat 10:39 and 16:35, Mark 8:35, Luke 9:24) through St Paul and Dante, to mention no others, which teaches that a great part of our present selves must die, must in some sense be burnt out, before our true selves can enter heaven. To live for ever unchanged would be Sartre's *Huis Clos*, it would be the fate of the Struldbrugs, those unhappy immortals in *Gulliver's Travels*. I must be changed, purged, transfigured, in order to enter heaven. I could easily have found all this in Christianity if I could have got on the right wave length; but in fact I received it first from agnostic writers on psychology such as Karen Horney, with her distinction of 'the neurotic personality' and the true personality, and then from the Hindus and Buddhists whose meaning escaped me entirely when I was young. I am almost sure that what I have got from Hindu philosophers is never precisely what they intend to convey, but the first contact of minds that have been so differently conditioned is likely to be blurred and imprecise.

If there is a purpose in the universe, we should be able to see man's place in a setting that is even wider than the totality of human life. This is what Teilhard de Chardin and the ethologists such as Konrad Lorenz have helped me to do. What we are learning about the psychology of animals helps us to understand ourselves, and the animal side of our nature is by no means to be despised. It is not true that we have a spiritual side and an animal side to our natures, which are respectively good and bad. That which is spiritual can be bad and that which is animal can be good.

From Teilhard I get a picture of ever-increasing evolutionary complexity from the hydrogen atom through the carbon molecule to the simplest forms of life and on to more complex forms of life in which man forms 'the leading shoot'. At every stage there is a coinherence. All life is bound together in the biosphere, through the interdependence of all species, the balance of nature. The world of human consciousness has an emerging unity. By our thoughts and feelings we affect each other in ways that are obvious and also in ways that are less obvious, and this intercommunication has been becoming closer in the last hundred years. The fact that the world is round makes it certain that, if we travel far enough, we shall meet. But the coinherence of human life requires a summing up in a further integration in some more organic relation of each to all, I believe that Christ came to give the human race its true unity, a unity which starts with the Church. That is the basic reason why the present disunity of the Church is a scandal. Christ will come again, but the manner of his second coming may be as surprising as his first coming in a manger. When he does come the unity of mankind will be consummated. This is something that we can only descry dimly, but the scriptural metaphors of the body, the vine, and the flock give us enough to go on.

Teilhard makes sense of life on earth but he says nothing about outer space. That was not his subject, but in this age a system that does not make sense of the galaxies does not make sense at all. There is here a glaring gap in theology. Dante in the *Paradiso* gave a beautiful and coherent account of all that was known of outer space in his day, and I am sure that any new theology of the cosmos must start from Dante, improbable as that may seem at first sight. But Galileo shattered the crystal spheres of the Ptolemaic universe, and since then we can no longer take the *Paradiso* literally. Soon Pascal was to write: '*Le silence éternel de ces espaces infinies m'effraie.*' The music of the spheres had grown silent. It was as if the Church had evacuated outer space, and the strange thing is that in more than 300 years no attempt has been made to develop a theology of Newtonian or Einstinnian outer space, to take the place of the older theology of Ptolemaic outer space.

I should like to know where heaven is, but it does not worry me that I do not know. I believe that there is a world we do not see as well as a world that we do see, and that the Church in heaven and on earth is one. We do not easily perceive the other world because our faculties and perceptions are evolved primarily for life in this world. But those in the other world appear to be aware of us. I do not know the mode of their existence but I suspect that they live in another system of time and space which is totally distinct in the material sense from the four dimensional continuum of space-time in which we live. They may experience more dimensions than we. Their experience of time is likely to be of a different kind from ours. Perhaps they experience time only as eternity, the simultaneous possession of a whole, to follow the classical definition of eternity.

The little we know does indicate that life in heaven will have analogies with life on earth. We are led to expect that we shall have bodies, though bodies that are freed from our present limitations. Heaven is in some sense a city and in some sense a feast. The mediaeval writer of the hymn 'Jerusalem the Golden' speaks of 'social joys' (*socialia gaudia*). In J. M. Neale's translation it runs 'I know not, O I know not, what social joys are there'. If I speak of heaven, what do I say of hell? One thing that is certain is that God respects our freewill. I shall not go to heaven unless I want to be with God. When I look into my heart, I see how difficult that is, and I cannot ignore the warnings of scripture. Nor can I ignore the possibility that one may live one's life in such a way that the sight of God would be unbearable. *The Screwtape Letters* and *Huis Clos* are a better guide to the *inferno* than Dante. If one goes to hell it is because one has chosen hell. God is merciful. I hope that hell is empty but I cannot conceal from myself the possibility of going there.

The perspectives of Christian belief are infinite, but God's manner of working is concrete and particular. He redeems the whole by starting in a particular place. Abraham, Jacob, the Jews, and the Church are chosen in turn, not for themselves but for the sake of mankind. Not for any virtue in themselves but so that they may learn the Tao and teach it to others. The earthly life of Jesus is the hinge of history on which everything turns. I do not understand in any clear sense how he delivers us from our sins. I cannot make much sense of any theories of the atonement but I know from experience that he does deliver us and I believe that his transfiguration was a foretaste of the destiny prepared for us, too. 'He became what we are, that we might become what he is', in the words of St Athanasius.

If you believe in Christ the question whether the Church will survive is not a real question, for 'the gates of hell shall not prevail', but it is quite possible that the Church will take some altogether different form in the future. I do not in fact expect any violent break and I am not greatly impressed with any suggestions that I have seen for a 'new form of Christian presence in the world', but I believe that there is a close analogy between God's ways with Israel in the Old Testament and his ways with the Church. We are going through a time of turmoil and I expect that the Christianity of a hundred years hence will be as different from the Christianity of 1900 as Judaism after the exile from Judaism before it.

If I look forward with hope and confidence, that is not because I think the forces of evil are weak. This is a bent world. We are not what we were meant to be. Something has gone wrong. The selfishness of the self is enough to explain the Fall, however that is to be understood, and it is a sufficient source for most of the evil in the world. In a fallen world we pull each other down in a 'solidarity of sin'. But the Devil also plays his part and his cleverest trick is to convince us that he does not exist. The religion of the Cross is not sentimental and should not be sentimentalized. Evil is real and suffering is real but in some way God makes all things work for him in the end. On the Cross God shared the suffering of the world and transformed it. The Christian faith is the only religion which makes suffering into something positive. I cannot explain in words how this can be, but when I gaze on the Cross I see that it is true.

God is working his purpose out, and I have said something about what I believe concerning his more general purpose, but he also has a particular purpose for each of us. It is only by degrees that I am becoming aware of Providence in my own life, but I do now see that things that have happened to me, and things that I have been given to do, have prepared me for what I was to do and to be later. It now seems to me that I began to live in quite a new way when I began to believe in Christ. I would almost say that before that I was playing at living. I would not say that my life is more spiritual, but rather that it is more real. Indeed I am almost Marxist in my suspicion of distinctions between the spiritual and the material. St Gregory Palamas wrote: 'If the body is to share with the soul in the ineffable blessings of the age to come, it is certain that it ought to share in them, so far as possible, from now.... For the body also experiences divine things when the forces of passion in the soul are, not by any means put to death, but transformed and sanctified.' I believe in the resurrection of the body, not in the immortality of a discarnate soul. I look for the remaking or transfiguration of the whole man.

The means for this is a perpetual wrestling with God. The mysterious story of Jacob's wrestling with the angel is a pattern for all Christian life. It is only thus that I begin to understand how prayer can be effective. God lets us wrestle with him as a human father lets his son wrestle with him in play. There seem to be two reasons for that. This wrestling with one's father is an actively loving relation, and it is the only way that we can strengthen our muscles for what lies ahead.

HYWEL D. LEWIS

was brought up in North Wales and is the son of a Presby-
terian Minister. He studied at Bangor before going to
Oxford. He became Professor of Philosophy in Bangor, he
has been a Visiting Professor at Bryn Mawr College, a
Fellow of Jonathan Edwards College, and visiting Lec-
turer at the Centre for the Study of World Religions at
Harvard. He is now Professor of the History and Philo-
sophy of Religion and Dean of the Faculty of Theology in
the University of London, and Fellow of King's College.
He has been President of the Mind Association, the Aris-
totelian Society and the Society for the Study of Theology.
He is Chairman of the Council of the Royal Institute of
Philosophy and Editor of the Muirhead Library of Philo-
sophy and of Religious Studies. *He is at present giving the*
Gifford Lectures in Edinburgh.

Among his books are Our Experience of God, Freedom
and History, Morals and Revelation, The Philosophy of
Religion, *and* World Religions *(the last jointly with R. L.*
Slater). He is the Editor of Contemporary British Philosophy *and* Clarity is not Enough. *He is also the author of*
several Welsh books, including a volume of poetry.

HYWEL D. LEWIS

I believe that God is. That, one may think, is an odd way to put it; and so indeed it is. One might have said, with the Creed, 'I believe in one God', or 'I believe there is a God', or 'I believe that God exists'. But to say 'I believe *in* God' is to go a good deal further than I want to go at this point. To speak of 'one God' might also imply that I thought it possible or conceivable that there should be more than one. I certainly do not think this, and I do not think that anyone else could do so once he had properly grasped what is meant by 'God'. To say that God exists might likewise be taken to mean that I could think of God without thinking of him as existing. This is one reason why some people expressly forbid us to affirm that God exists. But that, I much fear, is apt to mislead in other ways. It could suggest that God is not any kind of reality; and that, in my view, is disastrous. All of which shows, at the start, how very difficult it is to find a satisfactory way to refer to God and speak about him. I shall say more about that in a moment. But in the meantime let me be content just to say that God is, and if someone likes to substitute 'God exists' or 'must be', or 'is real', I shall not, for my own part, have a very serious quarrel with him here.

Let me now add that I hold this belief with absolute certainty. That is, I never doubt it when I think seriously about it. On the other hand, it is, alas, only too true that this belief does not have the central and dominant place in my life which such a belief ought to have. To believe in God should affect one's perspective on everything else, it should rid one of anxiety and make one patient and long-suffering at all times, it should fill one's life with joy and rid one of despondency and gloom. This, I fear, is far from being the case. If I say that I never doubt that there is God I must not be taken to claim great saintliness for myself. My life is not filled with the radiance which a belief in God should bring. That is because this belief is clouded over and obscured by many other things, it is shut away in recesses of my mind and not given its proper chance to dominate and change my other thoughts and attitudes. It is intermittent in this sense, quite remarkable so when one thinks what sort of belief it is, but not in the sense that I ever doubt it. The truth is that we have, as human beings, an astonishing ability to push certain things, about which we have no doubt at all, out of our thoughts and attention for much of our lives. That is part, at least, of what Newman meant in a famous distinction between 'real' and 'notional' belief. We believe things in a notional way when we have no doubt about them but do not allow them to mean very much to us, to come home to us, or, in the idim of today, to register. I read in the papers about Vietnam or about a famine in India, and we have no doubt much concern about such things, if we are serious-minded at all. But they do not upset and distress us like the Aberfan disaster. That was closer to us, we were able to picture it more vividly, it came home to millions of people as such disasters do not always do. If we knew the place, or if we had friends or relatives lost in the tragedy, or if we lived under the menace of a similar calamity, it would be still more real. But this does not mean that we seriously doubt what we read of other disasters or of sickness or famine in other more remote times and places. There may be very little reason to doubt the substance of the report, it is simply that we manage to push the thought aside, and in large measure this is inevitable if we are to live in the world and maintain our sanity. We cannot bear all burdens or allow all things to make their full impact on us. This is, all the same, an aptitude which we may exploit, or behind which we shelter, to avoid facing up to irksome facts or duties; and it is surprising how, in other ways, we can maintain a curious indifference to many things which we do not seriously doubt. We all know that we shall die, and that quite soon, but many people manage to get along, for a great part of their lives, as if this were not at all the case for them, not in the sense that they are not morbid, but in the sense that this knowledge has no real place in their thoughts at all. This is what often happens also to the belief in God.

That is one reason for the importance of preaching and prophecy, and for private and public religious observances. They help to revive and enliven what is dim and feeble. But it would be wrong to suppose, as some apologists do, that everyone has at least a dim belief in God. There are many, most of all today, who appear not to have such a belief at all, and it is idle to pretend that they do. To return to my main point, I find that, for many reasons I do not allow my beliefs about God to fill my life as they should do. But this is not mainly due to doubt; and I certainly do not doubt my initial belief that there is God. I do not for a moment think that here would be anything at all, or that anything could persist for an instant, unless there were God. This seems to me crystal clear, and I never have any doubt about it.

I have not in fact ever known it otherwise. I was brought up in a religious home and I seem to have been aware of the all-encompassing presence of God from as early as I can remember. 'Indoctrination', then, some will say, 'conditioning', 'you have only seen one side of the picture'. I must hasten to add that nothing seems to me further from the truth. My upbringing was an easy and liberal one, both my parents being gifted and intelligent. My father won open scholarships in mathematics at both Oxford and Cambridge at the same time before he 'lapsed' (as some foolishly put it) on completion of a course of unusual promise in mathematics at Oxford into the ministry of the Presbyterian Church of Wales. Out of meagre resources he acquired a very good library and was always borrowing new books. My brother and I had a very free run of the study and often did our homework there. We sat in on discussions between my father and his friends, sometimes late into the night. Religion was never forced upon me, I just imbibed it. Only once was I forbidden to read what I liked – a peculiarly blood-curdling thriller was taken from me when I was very young, only for me to find my father, to both our intense amusement, deep in it himself a little later. Chapel filled much of our lives, but then chapel was many things, entertainment and some riotous fun among them. Out of school, my time was little organized and I was free to roam the countryside at will.

I was familiar with Christian ideas early, but not in too rigid a doctrinal form. My main impression of early years, so far as religion is concerned, is more like the sense of a profound and entrancing mystery in all things so movingly described in the first pages of what I regard as one of the finest of all English books, Pater's *Marius the Epicurean*. As my love of poetry, which

I

developed early both for Welsh and English poems, took form, some sense of an enchantment and almost unbearable mystery at the heart of things made me a very responsive reader of Wordsworth and of Welsh poetry in the same vein, though more studied and chiselled in form. I have always been profoundly grateful that my religious life began in this way.

With adolescence and more maturity there came questions and reflection of a more sophisticated sort. Like most youngsters I was worried about the problem of evil and the seeming finality of death. The war books which began to appear in spate about this time disturbed me profoundly. There were also doctrinal diffi-culties, sharpened by forms of Barthian theology, much in the air at the time and finding its way, most unnaturally I have always thought, into the Welsh pulpit and discussions in the manse and ministers' room. My father paid little attention to it, but I was quite shocked and repelled by it. I have always remained pro-foundly averse to Augustinian doctrines of sin and guilt and bit-terly resent unreason in religion. When I first begin to write about religion, which was not my first interest in philosophy, my work was in sharp and angry opposition to much traditional theology.

At the same time two things became apparent to me. Firstly, that the sense of there being God became more irresistible the more I thought about it. Moving, as Plato in his great wisdom thought mental development should, from an unformulated sense of truth to a rational grasp of it, I found myself more certain than ever of the being of God. At the same time I had a deeper grasp also of what seemed to me to lie behind the doctrinal affirmations which I found, in so many respects, repellent in themselves. The more I thought about the teaching and person of Jesus, the more I marvelled. It had an appropriateness at all levels, something almost uncanningly unnerving, not least when most unexpected, which seemed right out of this world while yet, in all ways, in the midst of it. I was set pondering much on incarnational questions, and found in much of a highly gifted and inspired kind that I heard in the Welsh pulpit, still not far removed from its remarkable heyday at the turn of the century, and in the moving subtle sim-plicities of the Welsh hymns (rarely approached in my view for profound insight into Christian truth), the reality which had be-come a shadowy and sinister distortion in much popular thought and theological work. The result of reflection for me was to make religion more explicitly centred on the work and person of Christ, while fully understanding how repellent the account of this may seem in disertion and travesty.

The first of the main convictions I have noted is not a peculiarly or exclusively Christian one. The Hebrews had it long before Christ, and their grasp of just what it involved and how it should be handled, is one of the perennially astonishing features of early culture. But the sense of a supreme, essentially mysterious and elusive, all-encompassing reality, is of course at the heart of other great religions and becoming more and more to be thought to be a feature of worship elsewhere. The magnificent work of Rudolf Otto, classical in its simplicity as in its grasp of essentials, turned the tables on animists and others who, sometimes with naive assurance and lack of reflection on the evidence, spoke of a wholly natural origin of religion. That work has been much confirmed in subsequent thought and study. Otto's is not the last word, but he has set us on the right lines.

The sense of the holy, or, as I have put it, of a supreme, all-encompassing reality, must not be thought to be some kind of nature mysticism or pantheism. It is not centred on the world of nature but on what is thinly veiled in the world of nature and altogether beyond it. It can be sharp and luminous although it may be also blinding and stunning. It is never, as some have thought, neutral, even at the most incipient stage, in the sense that it is a further question whether it should be described in a secular or in some other way. It has always a reference beyond and must not be confused with any poetic impressions we may have of things, however illuminating those may be in their way. It may be close to art and poetry but is not the same. Religious insight is always transcendent.

Of the way this insight comes about, or of means of eliciting it, much may be learned from other religions than the Christian one. This is one important reason for the study of those religions. Even for the Christian who has in the Bible an unrivalled indication of the way God is 'without' and 'within', there are slants on this very theme elsewhere which can much deepen his understanding and enrich his experience. The Hebrew idea of 'creation', not dimmed in the least by its mythical forms, can itself be illumined from other sources; and those whose response to the Bible and to Christian witness is deadened by distortions of its meaning or the wrong sort of familiarity, may well find the freshness and initial insight they need in other religions. There is this special reason therefore why Christians should encourage the study of other religions. It is not the only reason, and I have, in this and in other ways, been anxious to further the renewal of both popular and scholarly interest in the study of religions today.

We may also be much helped here by recent philosophy, somewhat odd and surprising though that may appear. For in the encounter with recent empiricism and the more sceptical forms of linguistic analysis, religious thinkers have arrived at a new and more subtle grasp of the transcendence of God and the way this is known. They have understood that God is not to be characterized like other entities, that predicates are not affirmed of him as of other things. For the way in which we see that God is bound to be, the inevitability of God, also puts him outside the reach of ordinary discourse and analysis. God cannot be one term in a relation, for the way we are initially forced to think of him is through the essential inadequacy or incompleteness of all ordinary thought. The more we explain things in a rational way, the more we are aware of the limits of reason and the need for explanation, not by relating this to that, not by finding a place for things in a system, but in some way of which nothing more, from the nature of the case, may be said beyond positing such an explanation, an explanation of the way things are in normal understanding or of there being anything at all. There is a sense in which nothing could just happen to be, but to meet this requirement we have to posit an explanation of things which does not consist in further information or understanding, which is not an answer to any ordinary question, but is rather just the recognition that beyond the whole system of finite things and terms in relation, there is some Reality which is complete and self-subsistent as nothing else can be, a Reality involved in this way in the being of everything else, but in all other regards altogether mysterious in its essential nature. It is a mystery we recognize but never fathom.

It is evident that this is a peculiarly difficult idea to handle, not because of complexities within it, but because it is so hard to say enough without saying too much. In meeting the challenge to be explicit, to say what considerations weigh with them or are relevant, what counts for or against, some philosophers of religion today have developed exceptional skill in presenting, with the right amount of caution and positive affirmation, the essential mystery and reality of God. Professor E. L. Mascall, in a minor classic *He Who Is* and C. A. Campbell in *Scepticism and Construction* and *Selfhood and Godhood,* provide different but complementary examples of this. So does Austin Farrer in *Finite and Infinite.* But their ideas are not of course new, they go back through Kant and Aquinas to Plato and earlier, and this can hardly be the place to trace their course properly or unfold them further. Reflections of my own on this theme may be found in my paper *God and Mystery.*[1]

What philosophers say in this way about the perfection and elusiveness of God, about His transcendent supremacy and His mystery, is what the scriptures of great religions have also said very movingly. God is 'a God that hides himself', 'no man hath seen God', he is the 'One who is' but whose name even may not be properly known, or we give him a 'thousand names' because none will do. This is within the reach, or may break upon the mind, of the most untutored person as of the most sophisticated. Our initial hold of it is not a part of our intellectual skill, it falls outside it, although there can be superb intellectual skill in the refinement of our placing of it. This is where we also see the true import of the famous traditional proofs of the existence of God and of variations on questions of beginning and end in space or time. The being of God is not strictly proved in these ways, but familiarity with the proofs and a grasp of where they fail and also of what makes them attractive, may evoke or enhance the sense we have of the inevitability of the being of God and his essential mystery.

In an age of growing sophistication it becomes increasingly important to exhibit, in the way I have outlined, the way we are to think of God and to seek him. Many become atheists because they look for the wrong thing or in the wrong way. We have become especially conditioned, by the upheavals of our time and by

---

[1] *Prospect for Metaphysics*, ed. I. T. Ramsey.

social and other modes of culture, to look solely for what we can handle and, in principle at least, master exhaustively. This is commendable indeed at its proper level, but we need also to have a sense of what goes beyond all attainment at the ordinary level and is reflected back into it in refinement and enrichment. The postulation of any sort of bewilderment we please, or cultivated lapses into obscurantism or allusiveness, will not help; these just parody the true enterprise and bring it into ill-repute. Nor will it do, on the other hand, just to lower our sights and give an exhaustive account of religion, and of what we seek in it, in terms entirely of the 'here and now' of this world. That is the danger into which shrewd apologists are apt to fall, sometimes grievously as when, in presenting the elusiveness of God as more than one entity among others, as beyond prediction, they speak of him as some 'ground of our being' or 'depth' in some sense which identifies him with some dimension of our own being or of present existence. That is not the sort of hiddenness or elusiveness which God truly has. We must not compromise his transcendence in seeking to bring him within the orbit of men today.

Subject to that qualification it is of the utmost importance that thought about religion should be given full opportunity to open men's mind to what precisely they must be seeking; and, with growing sophistication, it is not likely that religion will thrive, least of all as true and healthy religion, unless thought has an increasingly important place in it; and the more it acquires that characteristic the more firm and secure will it be also. The renewal of religious thought and study in our own day is not only a good augury of a period of great, perhaps unparalleled, renewal of true religion, but also of a religion which will be marked by profounder certainties in the measure to which it has shed its dependence on dogmatic attitudes and false support. It has certainly been my own experience to have arrived at great certainty in proportion to my thought about my faith; and I am profoundly concerned to give a true impression to others of what may be gained in that way.

But this is not merely true of the being and mystery of God. There is much else in religion. Indeed it is not likely that religion has ever stayed or functioned solely at the level of a sense of transcendence, naive or sophisticated. That insight clothes itself at once and almost inevitably in others, and some religions have come in this way to make very bold affirmations about God. These need to be winnowed, to find what is truly religious and what is accretion due to particular states of culture and social existence – or to more fortuitous causes. But there is also the more inherent question of justification and of interpretation in new times and places. This is also a vital issue for today.

Nor is it merely so for the Christian religion. It is sometimes felt acutely in other faiths, and some non-Christian thinkers have said the most illuminating things about it of late, as in Sri Aurobindo's account of religious images and the authority of scriptures. But it is peculiarly sharp when historical claims are made of the sort we find in Christianity. The central problem arises very directly out of the very insistence on the essentially transcendent nature of God to which Christianity itself bears remarkable witness. For if God is so essentially mysterious and 'other' as this implies, how can anything at all be known about Him? Do we not contradict what we affirm him to be the moment we say anything? Does it not seem that the more religion is true to itself, the more it is itself bound to impede any move beyond an initial insight, does not the inherent logic of it condemn it to silence? Some have certainly thought so, and their religion has been a sort of silence. This deserves great respect when it is genuine and not, as it often becomes, an affectation many times removed from the insight and reverence which prompts it in the first place. But Christianity is above all a religion of the 'Word' and of the 'Word made flesh'. How can it vindicate itself if it is also a religion of 'the most high', the Eternal whom no man hath seen and whose ways are past finding out?

Only if it is firmly grasped that all knowledge of God, beyond the peculiar awareness that he must be, is mediated. It is in this respect not unlike our knowledge of one another, except that awareness of existence is also mediated here. I do not know my friend's thoughts as I know my own thoughts and sensations in having them. He is not a mystery to me in the sense of absolute transcendence. It is not that I have no idea what his thoughts and feelings truly are, but I only know them in some indirect way, normally at least by observing his body and hearing the sounds he makes. Even para-normal knowledge of others is not strictly direct. But this does not invalidate or impoverish the rich and intimate fellowships we have with one another. Communion is spontaneous and easy and the mediated character of it is usually quite unobtrusive and unnoticed.

Such also is our knowledge of God. We never, as the Christian specially insists, pass beyond our finite limitations and know divine being as it is in itself. We never get behind the scenes, if I may put it crudely, and see the 'mind' of God as it is in itself or hear the word not suited or muted to what we are. But how then does the mediation come about, how do I know what is genuine and reject the false, when does God speak and how is he heard? Are there not many voices, many scriptures, many revelations?

My own guide through the tangle of problems which this presents is found in what we find certain religious experiences to be. Religious experience is not being in a queer state or having paranormal awareness. It could involve this, but that is not what matters. What is distinctive of it is that the sharp renewal of the sense of the being and majesty of God invests the situation in which it happens with something of itself, it modifies the context which evokes it and induces a certain alertness and stillness of soul by which we have a much truer and more objective view of the world around us and of ourselves. This happens especially to moral insight, there is a refinement of it due expressly to the impact of the divine upon us. That does not give religious people a monopoly of ethical insight. Nor does it make them morally infallible. The divine impact is made upon us in the situation in which we find ourselves, including our attainments at the time. It will take time to have its full effect, and it may be distorted by errors of judgment or of fact which it may not immediately correct. The religious person is not relieved of the effort to improve his natural endowment and use it effectively. He has to wrestle like others, and in large measure in the same ways, with problems of moral perplexity. He must refine his moral sense and be as well informed as he can about the facts. God speaks to us as persons, not as machines, and there can be no question of being taken behind the scenes, as it were, and shown the mind of God as it is for him or given a blue print or set of rules directly applicable to all situations.

All the same, by the impact of God on our minds in the way

indicated we acquire in the course of time some clearly defined impressions of the will of God for us and of his special concern for what we are to be as moral persons. God is involved in all things, but he writes his message for us, as it were, more specifically in some experiences from which we thus learn what he is like in his special relation to ourselves. He speaks within our own consciences, and we come to associate justice and mercy pre-eminently with him. We learn of his concern for what we are like. But it is not in moral insights alone that God discloses Himself. There are other modes of religious experience. We find God, for instance, peculiarly near or available in trouble or distress or in the rupture of personal relationships, especially when that is brought about by our own moral lapses and the guilt which stands between us and both men and God. There are surprising, and sometimes overwhelming and breath-taking, renewals of religious awareness when we least expect or merit it. And there builds itself up in this way also the sense of God as one who forgives, who restores, who seeks and reconciles.

Nor are the experiences in question sharply episodic or detached. They extend into others and modify our outlook and attitudes in other ways. There is also a pattern in their recurrence (as may be seen in many contexts besides Christian ones), which accentuates the parallel with our knowledge of one another. That is, in my view, a most significant feature of religion to which I paid special attention in my book, *Our experience of God*; and out of these patterned experiences, and the deeper appreciation of their significance, there have come also vivid and colourful figurative expressions which acquire an increasingly profound associative power as they live on from one situation and period to another. Such is a great part of the language of Scriptures, and it is thus not surprising that so much reverence is shown to the form as well as the substance of what has been said 'of old', or as the *Upanishads* put it, to 'the Ancient makers of the path', even when correction is also found to be needed in the light of completed experience and understanding.

There is no easy way of detaching the figurative language of religion from its inner meaning; and many misunderstandings come about in that way. The metaphors are allowed to harden, or they are taken out of their context and made the basis of credal affirmations developed in abstractions from the live experience which gave them meaning. Apologists and critics alike fall into error in these ways. This does not mean that we have no need of doctrines and creeds, but that these need to be handled very carefully and related to what has been alive and germinative in religious life in the past. Theology is a peculiary exacting creative enterprise. And in this, as on other matters mentioned here, there is much that religions may learn from one another.

On the ethical side of the processes to which I have alluded, two matters need to be mentioned. The first concerns the moral insights I have noted. These, as I understand them, make us aware of what is objectively or in an absolute way required of us. I believe, that is, in an objective moral order. But this is quite consistent with admitting, as I certainly wish to do, that what is required or obligatory varies with the circumstances, which may include other people's opinions. There is nothing viciously relativist in this. No one would normally blame me for drinking as much water as I like, but it would be monstrous to do that regardless of my ration in a boat of ship-wrecked people. Failure to hold these sorts of distinctions lead to much misunderstanding. It has much to do with the harshness with which some people give heed to moral rules and the ease with which others speak of 'situational ethics' as if there were no objective or abiding principles. There is something which various situations require in a moral way in themselves, what is inherently appropriate to do. No one can be sure that he always knows what this is, but that does not preclude us from having confident opinions or from coming to know of some insights built up in this way which have the special sanction of religion and the preciousness of being involved in God's disclosure of himself to us in personal dealings.

At the heart of morality is also the idea of responsibility, and just as I oppose subjectivist or relativist views of ethical standards, so I deplore the tendency of many today to undermine the idea of ultimate moral responsibility and the freedom of choice which it presupposes. Much of my own work has been concerned with this topic and the account we should give of moral choice. In the same vein I have opposed much in traditional theology which questions or obscures our freedom and accountability. It is here that the doctrinal mishandling of truth already mentioned is seen at its worst. That is, in my view, a crucial matter in theology today.

Among the Hebrews the patterning of profound religious experience took a distinctive form and linked itself closely to their national history. They became more conscious of what God was about, of what he is like and of his nearness in his impact on the minds and hearts of men. That determined the stance they took in the vicissitudes of their private or public fortunes, and that much affected their history. It is here, and not in more external miraculous interventions, even if these happened, that we see God properly in history; and it is here that we begin to see the uniqueness of the Christian religion. In other ways it is like other religions. But the experience of God became more shaped and patterned among the Hebrews, and in that process it was corrected and purified. It acquired a peculiar momentum and a linkage with history. This was an uneven process with many backslidings and misunderstandings which were sharply corrected by censure from within and the pressure of events from without. But in due course there developed among the Hebrews a sense of God's peculiar dealing with them in this way and of their participating in some process they only partly understood and which reached far beyond their own destiny.

It is this which came to its culmination in the events described in the Gospels and in what Christians sometimes describe as 'the work and person of Christ'. In him the process acquired a certain finality, although it continues to have novel ramifications by which it is further illumined. The records which give us this are fragmentary, and they present many problems of which Biblical scholars are acutely aware. But they seem to me distinctive and authentic enough in their context to give us a remarkable picture of a person whose life and teaching draws the whole process of divine disclosure into himself so completely, and in such a rounded way, that, confronted with him, we can no longer speak of one term among others in the process, of a peculiar genius and peculiar obedience, but of one who cannot be classified in this way at all and in whom holiness is such that it can only mean the immediate presence of God, although in a finite form endurable by men. We thus speak of 'Very God, Very man'. And while this is the most astounding affirmation one could ever make, and for that reason not to be lightly made – indeed never without a sense of its desperate, daunting nature –, it is the conclusion which sober reflection on the evidence, on what is mirrored in the earliest Christian experience as enlivened imaginations and profound obedience see it, makes inevitable for us. We do not wholly understand what we thus affirm, but we understand enough to see that this is the only affirmation we can make and that it must be taken, not as hyperbole or literary extravagance, but as sober truth.

Of the problems which this presents I cannot say more now. But I must insist that the truth apprehended in these ways is neither a matter of blind dogmatic affirmation nor of formal or abstract deduction. It is based on evidence, but the evidence must, as the Bible puts it, be 'spiritually discerned'. We must be in tune with it, not in the sense of being uncritical, but in the sense of being prepared to make considerable effort to stay, in thought and deed, in the world of the evidence. It is the truth we seek, but we come to it through sanctified imaginations and obedience. There is much to favour this today, as there is also a great deal to hinder it. There is no easy road to Christian understanding, and we must shun the delusions of 'the short way' in our private ponderings and in evangelical work.

In the further unfolding of what is accomplished for us in the coming of God in Christ, I would ascribe a peculiar place to a certain privacy or inwardness which is one unavoidable feature of all experience. This is much queried by philosophers today, and, in opposition to prevailing forms of behaviourism and materialism, I have thus to attempt a defence of experience as a non-observable process of which each person is aware in the first place in having experience. This internality and elusiveness of persons could not be otherwise. They are incidents of our finite nature; and they bear very closely on our major problems. They make possible, for instance, the moral choices mentioned already. It is also in failure to come to terms with the limitations of our finitude, and in thus seeking to know others as we know ourselves, or as God knows them, that many grave disorders come about. Such are the perversions, like sadism or extreme preoccupation with passionate excitation, of which we learn much today. But the main point for the Christian is that it is in being driven in on our own interiority, and being thus cut away from life-giving contact with others and concern for them, that wrong-doing has its most devastating effect on ourselves. Of the cumulative form this takes over the ages and of the way the 'work of Christ' provides the only ultimate liberation and reconciliation here, this is not the place to speak further. I can only add that when our situation is viewed imaginatively in this respect, the Christian talk about atonement and reconciliation, repellent when understood out of its context and juristically, becomes profoundly significant and relevant to our condition.

I believe further that there is to be found in this way something quite unique and indispensable in the Christian religion with which everyone must be brought into contact, in this existence or elsewhere, before he can attain in its fulness the destiny which God has intended for us in fellowship with him. There is no substitute for the peculiar Christology of the Christian religion, and it must not be confused with faint imitations of itself elsewhere. It is no service to Christianity or to other religions, it is not tolerance but confusion, to suppose that we can have a Christology without the Jesus of the Biblical records, the Gospels and the New Testament as a whole.

In these respects I remain a dogmatic theologian. But the dogma must be apprehended in live experience and insight and in close relation to present situations. To dispense with its credal content, or to reinterpret it entirely in social or secular terms, will be fatal for Christianity. I have put this elsewhere in terms of a comparison with Rousseau's views about aristocracy. He said that aristocracy is the worst kind of government and the best form of government, it depends which kind you have. So with dogmas. They may be crude or revolting (and that is how many young people see them today) or they may be our pointers to what is most vital in our faith. Nor is it merely a question of what dogmas we hold or consider essential, it is quite as much a matter of the way we view and apprehend a dogma, or know what dogma means in religion.

I have no space to show what this further involves for questions like those of evil and immortality. I do not think we can ever have an exhuastively rational solution of the problem of evil, in the sense of being able to show, even in principle, how all things work for good. But I believe that we have sufficient independent grounds for our faith to be able to stand the tension of this situation and even to be tempered and strengthened by it. I also hold the belief in life after death to be an essential ingredient of Christianity, however hard it may be for us to envisage our survival of the dissolution of our bodies. There is much, on both these counts, which must remain dark to us now and be accepted in faith, faith that is not blind but firmly founded.

I must add that on many central affirmations of the Christian faith, and especially in grasping what is truly meant by 'the work of Christ' and the situation to which it is addressed, much light is thrown by general literature and especially by drama and fiction of today. It is not that such works always present, even in disguised form, what the Christian also holds. To say that would be to lapse into that attenuation and concession to prevailing fashions of thought to which I have myself sharply objected. But there is far more than we realize, in profound and gifted works of recent literature and even in the language used there, which says just what the Bible says. Much the same situations are disclosed, the same tensions, longings and aspirations exhibited. If only the Bible were better understood and read with more intelligence, and, if those who are put off by what they take religion to be, pondered more deeply what they may find in recent literature, the attitude of many to religion today would be changed. I believe in fact that the present secularization will be arrested and reversed before long, giving place to new and more triumphant forms of Christianity.

This will be marked by more complete and uncompromising loyalty to practical Christian ideals, and it will be better understood that Christian societies depart from the practice and spirit of charity at their utmost peril. This will be one of the lessons learned in a provisional period of secularization. On the credal side, not to be divorced from the other, major conceptions will come to be understood more on the basis of personal relations. And it is here that I find myself peculiarly favoured, as a Welshman, in having for my devotions and reflections so much inspired literature, and above all the hymns I mentioned earlier, in which the closeness of our personal involvement with Jesus is the central theme. I wish more could be quarried from this source and made available for others.

HAROLD LOUKES

was born in Sheffield in 1912, *educated at the Central Secondary School for Boys, Sheffield, and at Jesus College, Oxford. He then taught English in the University of Delhi and in a number of schools, until he joined the Oxford Department of Education, becoming University Reader in Education in* 1951, *and a Fellow of Jesus College. His publications include* Friends Face Reality, The Quaker Contribution, Secondary Modern, Teenage Religion, *and* New Ground in Christian Education. *He married Mary Linsell in* 1937 *and has four children and three grandchildren.*

HAROLD LOUKES

It ought to be possible, I suppose, to reach for a pen, write firmly I BELIEVE ... and then carry on with the various objects of the verb. But for myself, I am pulled up short by the verb itself, and the question, What am I doing when I 'believe'? And as I stop here, I am pushed back to the subject of the verb: this 'I': who is *he* when he is 'believing'? Does what he believes really matter to anybody else?

My trouble, so to speak, was that I was brought up 'Christian', and when I talk to my friends who weren't, and find that they don't 'believe' as I do, I say to myself, Is this all just luck, then? And is 'God' just a function of home life? Can we settle for the notion that beliefs are simply the result of one's education, like tastes in food and clothes and ways of speech? Do we say 'I happen to believe ...' just as we say 'I happen to prefer ...'? It is, quite simply, *worrying* that the world should look a different shape to people brought up in different kinds of home. If a belief is true, ought not most sensible people to recognize it? And *per contra,* if beliefs are as variable as they are, then are they not simply matters of taste, like brands of tobacco?

Those who brought me up would have been pained and shocked by these questions, and would have gone about whispering gravely that here was someone 'having doubts'; and they couldn't, they would have implied, say worse than that. They preached at me, I remember (how could I forget?) with solemn poetry and grave fluency, about 'truths' I had only to receive, embrace, accept. They *knew,* I was assured: they knew the God they spoke of, they knew the Risen Christ in their lives, they were personally and continually guided by the Holy Spirit. If it were not so, they said, they would have been terrible people.

In fact, they were rather nice people, most of them, and they impressed and moved me. But despite all this, and my own eagerness to receive and accept, *I never knew what they were talking*

145

about, nor what I was singing about in those hymns that brought
such a lump to my throat; nor what I was doing when I joined
fervently in those prayers. For a time I took it all very modestly,
and assumed it was all my fault. I had a bad spiritual ear, as it were.
It would all come in time. Or perhaps my moral life had to be
sorted out first. What I did not suspect at the time was the possibility that they did not know what they were talking about either.

But two things set me wondering. First of all, I discovered I
could talk like this myself. I found I had the gift of the spiritual
gab. I did not (I hope) lay claim to special revelations, or tell any
real lies about it all, but I did occasionally say more than I knew
for myself. And people seemed to like it. And then I went to teach
in India, and found men speaking with the same sense of conviction and same impressiveness from the same depths of personal
maturity, but in a different religious language and about different
gods. 'Then what were *they* talking about?' I asked. What were
we *all* talking about?

In the meantime I had found my way into the Society
of Friends, partly by chance, because I ran into some Quakers
and liked them and found myself working with them on problems
of common concern; and partly because Friends somehow 'set
my bells ringing', and in particular this bell of 'knowing what we
were talking about'. It was not that they seemed to know, any
more than anyone else; but that what they did not know they did
not say. They did not ask me to say a creed, nor, what I had
found worse, sing those moving affirmations of salvation. 'I had
found a place,' as I was later to read in Caroline Stephen,[1] 'where
I might, without the faintest suspicion of insincerity, join with
others in simply seeking God's presence,' – waiting in silence
to find out what I was wanting to talk about.

Here I was facing something much deeper than matters of taste,
and the aesthetics of worship. This is at root the problem of knowledge, the problem of all problems, of how we know anything.
And it was no accident that Quaker worship should meet me at this
point, because it was at this point that Quakerism all began, in
the thrust to empiricism that marked the middle of the seven-
teenth century: Bacon's *Novum Organon,* Newtonian physics,

---

[1] *Quaker Strongholds,* London, 1890, p. 13.

the end of the belief in witchcraft, the founding of the Royal Society, and Samuel Pepys watching experiments with a glass of water and wax balls, and 'how these balls did seem double, and disappear one after another, mighty pretty'. In this scientific climate, the Quaker apologist Robert Barclay pleaded for religion to rest on evidence just as science did. 'Natural truths move the mind to natural assent,' he said;[1] so must religious truths. They must rely on experience that 'is evident and clear of itself, forcing, by its own evidence and clearness, the well-disposed understanding to assent, irresistibly moving the same thereto.' In other words, Christians must know what they are talking about.

I have never been under the illusion (and nor have Friends) that religious thinking could be conducted in the same way or with the same rigour as scientific thinking. Metaphysics is certainly different from physics; and the positivist philosopher who seeks to reduce it to physics is making a methodological blunder. For when he asserts that if a proposition cannot be verified in physical terms then it is non-sense, he is making a metaphysical proposition that cannot be verified in physical terms, and must therefore on his showing, be non-sense. He may well be entitled to argue that metaphysics is not philosophy, since the question here is simply, What is philosophy? But he cannot claim to have said anything at all if he claims that metaphysics cannot be 'done' at all, and has no rational content, simply because it cannot be 'done' like physics. The short answer is that nobody ever thought it could. Nevertheless, there is something appealing in the question, To what sense-data do we refer? even if the answer may be somewhat unsatisfactory. And there is something appealing in Barclay's demand for 'natural truth', and evidence that 'irresistibly moves'. Without this, our metaphysic *is* simply a chance affair, dependent on who taught us. We must somewhere, sometime, be able to recognize what people are talking about, or there is no point in listening to them.

Quaker worship thus seemed to me to start at the right point, in contrast with liturgical forms. The burden of the forms was, 'Start with what we say about God'. The burden of the Quaker meeting was, 'Start where you are and see what happens'. The

[1] *An Apology for the True Christian Divinity*, 1678.

liturgy said, 'Say these words after me'. The silent meeting said, 'Say nothing at all until you have to'. The liturgy said, 'Talk first, know later'. The meeting said, 'Look first, and talk only about what you see'. I have come to realize, over the years, that I was seeing this contrast too sharply. The liturgy is more *educative* than I had realized. It is really saying, 'say these words and then you will see their meaning', as a teacher might say, 'Learn this poem and then you will know what it means'. *Credo ut intelligam*, I have come to learn, has a certain validity, and the liturgy urges me to do just that. At the same time, I have discovered that the meeting for worship is less adventurous than I had thought. The silence is a silence of common assumptions; and these people who sit together, carefully refraining from directing each other's attention, start out with common attitudes already profoundly formed. A man and his wife in agony over a sick child do not need words to fill the silence of their anxiety, but they do need words to tell them how sick he is. A liturgy makes sense, then, even in a tough, empiricist climate, as an invitation to experience; and silence would make no sense without a degree of common understanding about what was going on. As I have discovered this, I have become free for all forms of worship so long as they are *worship*, and I look back on worship-moments in Cologne Cathedral, a Welsh Bethel, the Jama Masjid in Delhi, and beside an ashram-well with Mahatma Gandhi at his evening prayers.

But what is worship? What are we talking about here? Much of the Quaker meeting could be described without using the concept of worship at all, simply as psychological good sense. There is commonly a fair period of undisturbed quiet to start it all, in which the silence measurably deepens (literally measurably, for as the minutes pass people move less, they sit stiller, they breathe more quietly). And the individual feels himself growing quieter. The thoughts he brought in with him, pleasant or unpleasant (the frustration over a parking place, the little jest or good news from a Friend at the door, his feelings about the weather) tend to float off his mind. If he brings in a real anxiety he may find it does not float off, but he is still quieter, because he is aware of something deeper to attend to – as a road drill is annoying outside a concert hall, but one can reduce its power by concentration on the music. The presence of the others, silent too, helps the float-ing-off process, for there they are, with *their* thoughts and anxieties, but now still, reaching down to a deeper level. (And of course, we are talking metaphysics already, but since Freud talked the same kind of metaphysics we have an idea of what we are talking about when we speak of levels of consciousness; and it is not extravagant to suggest that this process of 'settling down', as Friends call it, is kin to the delving below the surface that goes on in the psychiatric session.) When the deeper level has been reached, and the meeting is 'gathered' (another significant piece of Quaker jargon), there is a curious sense of unity-in-the-silence. Friends are sometimes in the habit of describing this in terms of Jung's collective unconscious,[1] but for myself I have never understood what *he* is talking about, and I prefer to stick to the image of the anxious parents, whose unspoken common feeling goes down to the roots. They 'know each other in love', we might say: they know each other to be loving. And so the members of the meeting know each other to be going deep.

Not all meetings are 'gathered' in this way, but seasoned Friends usually know when it happens. And they recognize ministry from the depths: those taut, economical reports of findings from the silence, easily distinguishable from the little holy thoughts that come from the superficies. True ministry always seem apt ('speaking to one's condition' is a favourite Quaker commendation) to the moment: not to what was said last, but to where the meeting has got to in the time nothing has been said. And before the meeting is over the tension of being gathered has usually been released both in silence and words, the words themselves 'answering' each other, not as debates answer each other, but as the two sides of a concerto answer each other.

A positivist would no doubt attempt to find explanations for all this in psychological terms, but I find myself wanting to use religious language here: the sense of the presence of God, encounter with the Other, touching down to the ground of being, the thrust of the unconditional – these are all metaphors, and are no more helpful than metaphors can ever be, but they serve to convey something. I do not know much more about 'God' as a result of all this, but I would say that I have been reminded that

[1] Martin, P. W. *Experiment in Depth*, London, 1955.

anywhere, in any situation, I 'find God' in it only by 'going deep'; and that there is no situation in which God is *not* to be met in the depths.

My talk about 'God' is thus not so much talk about the divine nature, or the being of God (though it was in my early days, and a lot of nonsense I talked about it), so much as talk about 'meeting points'. It will often sound like talk about my own feelings, of course, because they are my side of the meeting point, and I can only give you my side. But then, if I were to try to convey how cold the weather was, I could perfectly properly describe my numb fingers and shivering form, and be taken to mean, 'I am meeting the cold.'

There seems to be two aspects of my meeting-point in worship that makes me want to say 'God' instead of 'psychology'. One is a sense of being on a frontier, somewhere beyond which I cannot see, but yet sensing a reality in the beyond. The other is a sense of being challenged, of meeting some sort of imperative that comes *at* me, that I haven't made up for myself out of my own education or dreams. Neither of these experiences has the hard certainty of Barclay's 'natural truth', or a modern scientist's evidence, but I find myself having to take them seriously, and I find that other people sense them too. And so it was that Kant set all my bells ringing with his 'Two things fill my mind with ever-increasing wonder and awe, the more often and the more intensely the mind dwells on them: the starry heavens above me and the moral law within me.' In this sort of language it is possible to speak of all life as worship, set about as it all is with awe and obligation, infinite and imperative. Without this language I cannot use the cliché 'Life is worship' at all, because in practice I do not go about worshipfully. I go about *busily*, making my plans, being in charge of myself, working things out, doing masterful deeds like driving cars and switching lights on and off and writing a chapter for a book and helping with the washing up. And all these I do most of the time without reference to the ultimate: I throw the switch because I know it works, with no thought for the mystery of electricity. Most of my life is lived, as it were, on the surface, without attention to the depths. But from time to time I am pushed to the frontier that I see in worship. Often this is when things go wrong (and this may be partly the reason why people suddenly go to church again in wartime). The switch won't work, and I am aware of 'electricity'; or my smooth human relationships are shattered by conflict and I am aware of hate in myself doing battle with love. Or sometimes it happens when things go unexpectedly right, and awe comes over me from the sunset or the stars: once, indeed, 'discovering' infinity in a mathematics lesson, and being made to *face* it, which is a rare event in a maths lesson. Or when I fall in love and eagerly reach out to accept obligations I hadn't dreamt of.

Now these are still experiences that the behaviourist psychologist can in principle 'explain', but I see in them meaning from the inexplicable. I am awe-struck by meaning, not by chaos; I am commanded by otherness, not by myself. So to the question, 'Does the world *mean* anything?' I answer, 'Yes', though I should be hard-pressed to say what I mean by meaning, and harder still to say what the meaning is. What I am sure of is that I want to look for it; and this wanting seems to me to bring meaning with it. When the orchestra begins to tune up, we do not listen for meaning. When it begins to play, even if the item is one of those experimental compositions that sound very much like an orchestra tuning up, we do listen. Even when we listen, we may still miss the meaning; but what is certain is that we shall miss it if we don't listen at all. 'Why do we have to live?' a young girl once asked me. 'To find out why we have to live,' I should say in reply.

This 'belief' is not an argument from evidence (and not in the least, for our generation, one of Barclay's 'irresistible natural truths'), but a choice. On conflicting evidence, order weighed against chaos, justice against injustice, beauty against desolation, rare moments of happiness and content against continuous days of alienation and despair, I still choose meaning: the choice that man is *for* the order and justice and beauty and happiness and content, even when he is suffering the chaos and injustice and desolation; just as I believe man is *for* health when I walk through a hospital ward where all are sick.

I respond, then, with a belief in intention. There is no possibility of 'proving' my response, but since there is no possibility of 'proving' an absence of intention either, this does not seem particularly worrying. We must choose one or the other, and this is my choice. And when this has once been said, we are talking about

'God', for 'intention' is inconceivable without 'intender'. I am not prepared to say much about the 'nature' of the intender, except that 'he is what he is', and he is to be met, awful and commanding.

My ordinary life, with its 'natural' truths, is thus stretched out between two points on the frontiers of knowledge: the starry heavens above, the mystery of the given, described nowhere better than in the last chapter of *Job*; and the demand on me to be and to act, to bring something into the system.

But what is the nature of the demand? What are we talking about here? 'The moral law within' smacks too much of an internalized set of moral customs that I have simply been taught to obey; and though most of my life dances to these strings (for I have neither time nor energy to think out every situation afresh, with a world perspective and an ultimate dimension) the shape of the obligation seems different from a set of mere customs. It is the obligation to be a person, to take hold of the conventions and to play my own tune on them, as a musician must learn first to 'get the notes right' and be faithful to the composer's spirit and intention and *then* bring something more from the depths of his own spirit. It is the composer's intention that this should be so, and that each performance should be a unique event.

In my moral playing, I fluff a good many notes, and getting 'the moral law' right according to the rules is a fair account of most of my moral effort. But I am conscious of the demand on me to try to do better than the rules: to make the rules 'sing' with my own unskilled but nevertheless personal voice. I am thus, in the end, a 'new moralist', though some of the discussion of the new morality frightens me to death. When people begin to talk about love, says the cynic, then is the time to ring up your solicitor; and I shrink from those who are on familiar terms with 'love' as much as I used to shrink from those who were on familiar terms with God. Even here, in the world of moral and personal values, I want to know what we are talking about: I want my metaphysics to come down at least to the physical frontier, and touch on some of the 'natural truths' I can point out to my friends.

The 'new morality' calls urgently for a rigorous effort of thought, not only about 'situations' but about the conventions within which we learn to be moral at all. The conventions are the language with which we speak to each other, and there is no other language available to us. And just as the new poetry is still in English, so the new morality is still in 'convention'. Of course language changes, becomes obsolete, is enriched by new words and idioms and cadences; and so do moral conventions. But there always remain some conventional things you cannot do: you cannot spell 'love' h-a-t-e, and then expect to make your way into a woman's heart.

This seems to me to be orthodox Christianity. If I read the Sermon on the Mount aright, Jesus was saying, 'You remember the law? Well, do *better* than that, but don't do worse.' The principle still holds: we have to justify breaking the conventions by reference to some principle that is more moral than they are.

But where are these principles to be found? Moral codes from other ages, whether Hebrew or Anglo-Victorian, are interesting but not binding: they are not even helpful in the really difficult areas of a modern industrial society. There are a few first-order principles one can advance, such as truth-telling and justice, on the grounds that life in society would be impossible without them. There are – and this may be nearer the mark – rational methods of thinking through situations (what are the consequences? for me? for the other? for all men everywhere?). But such laws and methods do not tie everything up beyond a shadow of doubt. And even where they seem to, they can still be followed faithfully but without compassion, and then they are useless.

And so we come back to love after all: but it must be tough-minded, not sentimental, not *feeling* at all, but willing on behalf of the other, of all the others. When Jesus spoke of plucking out an eye or cutting off a hand he was not, we should now agree, talking about asceticism as a way of life, but he *was* recognizing that love does not come easy: that right conduct is not just a matter of spontaneous life. It is splendid when it is, of course, but human nature is not to be trusted to be merely spontaneous. The stuff we are made of, if the psychologists are to be trusted, is pretty wicked stuff: a little lust, a little greed, a little pride, a little of each of the seven deadly sins. These are the things that make us tick, and it is with this unpromising material that we must learn love.

I have therefore no difficulty with the doctrine of original sin, which seems to me a simple statement of the case. But I share the

Quaker view that the sin is nothing to make a fuss about, and that it is the capacity for something better that matters: the light of Christ shining in every man. This is what we must set out to meet and to answer. This is why I was a pacifist in the last war. It is why I work in education. It is why I vote on the left (though many Friends don't, and it must be admitted that any attempt to represent a particular party as God's party will have to rest on some curious arguments). It is why I want to see good housing and town-planning and health-services and a friendly community life; for how can 'every man' see the light shining if he lives on a caravan site surrounded by disease and hostility? It leads me to be bothered about the developing countries and the East-West conflict with its absurd ideological abstractions and forgetfulness of the facts of human existence; and about food and population; and colour-prejudice; and all the other concerns of the good liberal. There is nothing very original about all this; and I cannot pretend that I make much contribution to it all except through my membership of the Society of Friends, which does.

'Membership of the Society of Friends' is not, for any Quaker, a matter of high doctrine, but of simple commonsense. Quakerism was seen at the outset, and is seen again today, as a movement rather than a church, and 'membership', though carefully arranged and recorded, is mainly a matter of knowing who may be counted on. I find this empiricist attitude congenial, and feel no need of metaphysics here. The facts are surely hard enough: the fact that we learn to love by loving and being loved; the fact that the private conscience is never sensitive enough alone; that the personal will is never strong enough alone; that the widely concerned individual can only specialize on one or two of his concerns and neglect the rest; that the specialist then gets things out of proportion, and begins to think that if we could only coddle all unmarried mothers or rescue all alcoholics or comprehensivize all schools the millennium would begin; the fact that social concern must take warmth and meaning from beliefs about human nature and its needs and potentialities . . . and so I could go on. If the church did not exist, it would be necessary to invent it, even today when it seems to be dwindling so fast in size and influence. The historic *tasks* of the church – education, welfare, and the rest – have been floated out to be steered by secular hands, so that 'the church' is now to be seen in trade unions and welfare services and government departments and Rotary, thoroughly mixed up with the secular. But despite all this, there is still need for some men and women to meet together carrying a concern for man as man, and not simply for men-on-probation or mothers-without-husbands or lonely widows. 'The world', in the old fearsome jargon, needs 'the church'.

And even if it were not so, there are those who need to worship directly, consciously; and who, if there were no church, would have to invent *something*. For neither Friends nor other Christians would that 'something' be exactly what they have: but this is to say no more than that we should none of us be the same without our history, which is not a profound observation. As it is, the history is part of what we should have to invent: even Quaker worship, as nearly formless as it could be, leans heavily on 300 years of practice. History carries its own awe, and power to humble, and becomes a harmony in the worship.

In a sense, then, I would, after all, claim a high doctrine of the church, and say 'God made it', if I may be taken to mean that the human condition needs a community for loving and worshipping, whose raison-d'être is to be turned outwards, to be used and spent and squandered; that such a community is part of the intention for humanity. And that even in the hygienic Utopia towards which we are supposed to be advancing, when *all* the welfare tasks are handled efficiently by a perfectly civil service, there will still be a need for men and women to meet for loving and worshipping.

Where my 'high doctrine' stops short is at any attempt to draw a metaphysical distinction between church and non-church. The physical distinction is simple enough: it is marked by members' lists, or lists of communicants, or of those baptized, or of subscribers to church funds. But as soon as we try to make metaphysical distinctions on the basis of these physical ones, or by any other recognizable criterion, we are in trouble. The distinction between 'saved' and 'unsaved' is no longer fashionable, but there still hangs about Christian thinking a shadow of this old dichotomy. There is thought to be a real difference between a 'Christian' and a 'non-Christian', which I find it difficult to identify. I do not find my humanist friends any 'worse' than my Christian friends, nor my Hindu or Muslim friends different in any way that I cannot explain on sociological or educational principle. They are made of the same human stuff, and they respond to awe and obligation in the same way as a Christian would. I am not here arguing that all men are equally 'good', which would be nonsense; but only that we cannot categorize, or predict in categories, on the basis of 'Christian' and 'non-Christian'.

Then do I, the Christian would ask at this point, 'believe' in Christ? And what am I talking about if I say that I do? If there is no necessary, predictable difference between 'Christian' and 'non-Christian', then is Christ 'necessary' at all? I should want – as will now have become apparent – to engage in a good deal of demythologizing of the records of the life of Jesus, from the birth stories to the resurrection stories; but I believe we have here a coherent and broadly faithful account of the kind of man he was. And I meet in this picture of him the awe and obligation at the central point of the human situation. He impresses me as 'beyond' the human, with a purity and totality of self-emptying beyond all other men's attainment, and at the same time 'within' the human, in the sense that he makes me feel that *that* is what I am *for*. For this experience of him I am ready to use the word 'divinity', and to share with other Christians the statement that he is unique.

But I am not ready to argue that in consequence I or his other followers have any sort of monopoly of insight or wisdom. I 'recognize' Christ when I see 'Christlikeness', even among those who have never heard of him, or having heard of him have avowedly rejected him; not when I hear him talked about. My conversation with non-Christians is therefore not 'message' but 'dialogue'. I want to ask them where they learnt what they show of love and insight and compassion; what is their experience of awe; to what they felt themselves to be 'obliged'. I shall *not* be saying, 'Whom therefore ye ignorantly worship, him declare I unto you', but rather 'Whom therefore we ignorantly worship, him declare we to each other'. For despite all the doubts and hesitations that I have to live with, I find a point at which I must declare myself. I am committed. Here I stand. And at this point I am untroubled: not knowing that I am 'right' and another 'wrong', but content to declare myself in a situation where I take another's declaration seriously, my word bringing out his word, his word bringing out mine. We are both 'wrong', for we both 'ignorantly worship'. But we are both 'right' if we are both 'declared'.

PAULINE M. WEBB

was born in Wembley, Middlesex, and educated all over the place. She is unmarried.

At King's College, London, she obtained B.A. Honours in English, A.K.C. Diploma, and a Teacher's Diploma. She taught at Thames Valley Grammar School, 1949-52, then joined the staff of the Methodist Missionary Society and later became its editor. In 1953 she became an accredited Local Preacher of the Methodist Church, and in 1964 took up an Ecumenical Fellowship for a year's study at Union Theological Seminary, New York, where she obtained the S.T.M. degree. In 1965 she was elected as the youngest Vice-President ever of the Methodist Conference, and is now Methodism's first Director of Lay Training.

She has written: Women of our Company, Women of our Time, All God's Children, Operation Healing, *and* Are we yet alive?

PAULINE M. WEBB

I first saw the slogan chalked up in large, uneven capitals on the grimy wall of the New York Subway at 116th St. and Broadway. 'GOD IS DEAD', it shouted, and in scrawled script underneath was added 'Signed by Nietzsche'. But someone had determined that that should not be the last word. By the side of the first slogan there was another: 'And now Nietzsche is dead – signed by God.'

Both statements seemed to me to express a great mystery. To say of a human being that he is dead is to say something far more than can be proved by physical fact. To be a human being is to be something more than a physically functioning body. It has to do with a total, purposeful striving after existence. It has to do with being a person and with being related to other persons. In other words it has to do with the whole mystery of 'being'. My schoolteacher who used to rap my knuckles if I wrote in my exercise book about humans without remembering to call them human beings was really teaching me something of very great significance. It is the 'being' that gives significance to life and the 'ceasing to be' that is the great mystery of death.

To say that God is dead is to say nothing that can be proved or disproved as a physical fact, any more than God's existence is capable of empirical proof. It is a statement that has significance only when we have decided what we mean by the concept 'God'. If by the word 'God' we mean that source of Being which lets everything else be, then to say that God is dead is to say that Being's source has ceased to be, so that the statement is one that we, as human beings, experiencing being, cannot make. If we go further and claim that the concept of God is concerned with that purposeful striving towards an ultimate Good, which seems to give meaning to the whole phenomenon of life, then to say that God is dead is to say that life itself has ceased to have meaning, which is what the nihilism of Nietzsche would seem to express.

159

Yet this very concept of nothingness is, as Heidegger puts it, 'a foil to Being'. Things that are are seen against the background of the abyss of nothing and cause us to wonder even more at the mystery of being.

So death, this inescapable mark of human finitude, is in fact the experience that raises all the questions about infinity. Because we know we must die, we must find out what it means to live. 'Thank God for death,' writes Hawthorne. 'It allows us to become ourselves.'

But I personally was in a much less philosophical mood when I first saw that writing on the wall. I needed at that moment not so much a philosophical interpretation of death as a faith that would make sense out of life. And like all the real questions that men ask, my questions were coming out of a deep, searching personal experience. I was returning home to college from Harlem, where I had been helping friends of mine prepare for a journey to Selma in Alabama, to share in the protest marches organized by the Civil Rights movement. A concern for racial justice has always been a passion of my life, and I was convinced that these men and women who were prepared to go and join in the peaceful demonstrations against racial discrimination had right on their side. Then had come the black, sad news. One of the demonstrators, James Reeb, a young Unitarian minister, had been stabbed. 'James Reeb is dead', they told us, and the horrible, sickening finality of it suddenly brought everything we were doing into question. What was the point of demonstrations of this kind if they were to end only in death and destruction? Was there really anything more significant than one man's life? Was it sense to believe that there is such a thing as a cause that is right which must continue the struggle even when evil seems too strong for it? Yet I came from that sad and bewildered meeting with one thing quite clear in my mind. Tomorrow I would join my Harlem friends once more, and we would be processing as we had planned down through the streets of Manhattan and we would be singing our song of faith in the face of death.

> 'We shall overcome, we shall overcome –
> Deep in my heart I do believe
> We shall overcome some day.'

Deep in my heart I do believe. That is really all there is to say. The slogans may tell me that God is dead and that men must die – but if I am to live and to make any sense at all out of living, then I have to believe that it all adds up somehow, that the things I feel so deeply are right are in fact part of the very purpose of God, that Being who so mysteriously, I would say, so graciously, lets me be.

So I begin by saying 'I believe in God', and for me this means I believe that Being has meaning, and that I have been given being in order that I may explore and experience that meaning in the fullest possible kind of life. This Being and this meaning underlie not only my own life, but all the life of men, and of nature, of the world and of the universe. It is that one Source of Being that makes it possible to speak of one universe, and life is a constant search for and discovery of that underlying unity of all things which enables us to understand their essential nature. And always this search for a unity is bound up with a search for perfection.

It impresses me deeply that human beings never seem content with things as they are, but are always striking towards things as they might be. Even a simple act like kicking a ball on a field becomes for human beings a great and intricate exercise in co-ordination of mind and muscle, in teamwork and strategy, in co-operation and competition so that what begins as a football game becomes a matter of vital debate for many thousands of men every week of their lives, as they decide whether or not it has been a 'good' game. By 'good' they might mean 'good for me' (I won money on it), or 'good for the team' (they came top of the league), or 'good for everyone' (a display of human skill and achievement). Or the simple matter of arranging flowers in a vase becomes an exercise in pattern and harmony of colour, an art that absorbs the energies and conversation of thousands of women rejoicing in the opportunity of sharing in the creation of a 'good' design.

It is as though human beings purposefully and meaningfully are continuing a process going on all the time around and within themselves, as the millions of cells which go to make up the physical structure, each so beautifully and intricately organized, co-operate with tremendous drive and purpose to fulfil their various functions, and even to change those functions efficiently if required. In the physical realm, we recognize health as the working together of all these things for 'good' – and disease as a disorder that ought not to be. In the social realm, we analyse the pressures driving men into social structures and we recognize that there are 'good' things in society, such as justice and order and peace which becomes the objects of our striving. In the aesthetic realm we accept that beauty and harmony are 'good' concepts which can be expressed in form or colour or line. In the moral realm we accept that we meaningfully speak of 'good' and 'bad' principles even though different societies and cultures may see different things as 'good'. Always we are reaching out to some kind of goodness, of perfection. And in all societies we recognize that what begins with a concern for 'what is good for me' (e.g. food, shelter, etc.) must develop into a concern for 'what is good for us' (e.g. life in society) and that the best of all is 'what is good for all' (e.g. world peace, racial harmony). One would have thought that the realities of the human condition, with its long history of repeated failure to attain to the good, would have eventually destroyed the image of goodness. Yet still we strive towards it, as though there were some Supreme Good setting the ultimate standard. And still we think of goodness in positive terms and evil in negative terms, as though the one were purposeful and the other destructive of true purpose. So this human striving after goodness posesses an even greater problem for the man who sees no meaning or purpose in life than the agonizing experience of evil and suffering poses for those who believe that the purpose is goodness, that God who lets us be is good.

To anyone who like me has grown up in Lancashire the phrase 'let us be' has deeper implications than its literal meaning. 'To let someone be' in Lancashire dialect is to allow them freedom to be themselves, to get on with the job of living without too much interference from beyond their own wills. This too seems to me to be a clear fact of human experience in so far as man's relationship to God is concerned. Man quite clearly is free to be himself and he constantly chooses for or against the Good. So the whole of his life is a series of decisions about the meaning and purpose of his life – whether he will go along with that creative energizing force which seems to me to be all the time urging him on towards goodness, or whether he will in fact refuse to accept the very purpose of life itself. If the infant does not turn towards life in its first efforts to breathe and to suck, to secure 'what is good for me', it will die. If man in society does not turn towards life in his striving after justice and political stability to secure 'what is good for us', community becomes chaos. If mankind does not turn towards life in seeking 'what is good for all', we know that the nuclear hope which opens up such great technological possibilities for the nations, so that at last we could really love one another and see all men fed and clothed and sheltered, could become the great nuclear disaster in which we utterly destroy each other. So there is set before us life and death – and it is in man's power to choose life that he may live.

Faith in God means for me the choice of life and the acceptance that positive good is its purpose. I realize that I was well 'conditioned' to a belief in God from my earliest years and that it would have been difficult to escape that conditioning. But the very fact that I am aware of this psychological process of conditioning does, I think, limit its force, even though I recognize its presence. My experience has been that I have been free to accept or to reject such faith, as I have been free to accept or reject various other kinds of conditioning that I received as a child. Some I have accepted because they were clearly essential to wellbeing – the habit of eating meals regularly and of observing the various conventions of polite society. Some I have rejected because they did not reflect my own later experience – my political views, for example, are not the same as my parents'. And for a time I rejected too the body of belief in which I was brought up. But the concept of God that I was given as a child was always presented in the context of a life to be lived rather than in things to be believed, and the quality of living, I recognized in my own home as something which stemmed from a life of faith became for me a quality I wished to emulate, and so to this extent I was conditioned towards belief. Added to this came the confirmation of experience as I met people I admired who seemed to me to have this same quality of a positive acceptance of goodness as a way of life which they expressed in terms of faith. It seemed to me eventually, after long intellectual arguments with myself, that I could not think of any better way of life than this way of faith and I could not tolerate the thought of anything less. I wanted to share all the concerns of the humanists, but to go much further than they do in recognizing that the human values are also the ultimate ones.

All this can only be fully expressed for me as I go much further than saying 'I believe in God', and begin to say 'I believe in Jesus Christ'. The God in whom I believe is the God who stands behind Jesus – the God who has made the purpose and meaning of life clear to me in the form I can best understand it and receive it, the form of a person. In this man all the best of which human life was capable was epitomized. It does not seem possible to me that anyone could have 'invented' Jesus. To question his historicity seems rather like saying that if William Shakespeare did not write his plays, they must have been written by someone else of the same name. My sister used to say that if the New Testament writers invented the Person of Jesus, they were such geniuses that they deserved to get away with it! Pilate's 'Behold the Man' summarizes what the Incarnation really means, that this is what men are meant to be like. This has such deep implications that the mind almost fails before them. For one thing, it means that the turning outwards from oneself in love to others is quite literally a turning to the ultimate 'goodness' which is God. Conversely, a refusal to do this is a refusal of the meaning of our being and quite literally death to the individual. It also means that society as a whole, from which we received by the process of 'socialization' our ideas of goodness, is the means through which we are to grow in likeness to Christ, so that whatever hinders human growth in social structure is against the ultimate goodness, which is God. So there can be no distinction between sacred and secular. This is uncomfortable, because it would be much less bother to be able to enclose oneself in a nice 'sacred' envelope, but this is surely impossible if one really believes in the Incarnation. If one can believe in it, there can be no question of whether 'religion is about social justice', because the religion of Jesus could not really be about anything else. Nor can there be any questions about whether it will all make sense in the end – whether we shall overcome one day – , because the faith in Jesus is the faith that everything is in fact summed up in him and that he is the one who has already overcome even death itself.

I suppose that Pilate felt a certain air of finality when he signed his proclamation 'Jesus is dead'. And yet every Sunday, 2,000 years later, I and 750,000,000 other Christians assert that I believe that this Jesus 'suffered under Pontius Pilate, was crucified, dead and buried; on the third day He rose again from the dead and ascended into heaven, from whence He shall come to judge the quick and the dead.' I can do no other than believe that the God who is the Supreme Good raised Jesus from the dead and thus vindicated all that he had been and done and said among men. In the words of Geoffrey Ainger, in his book *Jesus Our Contemporary*, 'Down the centuries echoes God's great Credo . . . "I believe in this man, Jesus of Nazareth." '

So faith for me is primarily an attitude of commitment to Jesus, a decision that that Man who lived in Palestine 2,000 years ago is God's Word to every man, everywhere, for all time.

I felt this come home to me very forcibly recently in the most realistic Biblical film I have ever seen – Paolo Passolini's production *The Gospel According to St Matthew*. In this film Jesus was portrayed as a real man, living among a rough peasant people, a man of strength and energy, a man always in a hurry, a man whose presence brought health to the sick but threatened disturbance to the complacent, a man who blazed with anger at the hypocrites and melted into laughter with the children. We watched him for two and a half hours striding across our screen, knowing just where he was going and intent on getting there quickly. He looked to me less like the pale Galilean of Western tradition and much more like some ardent and energetic young man of contemporary Africa. But his ardour was one of a burning love – a love made real in his deeds as much as in his word. Then came the tragedy. We knew there could be no other way. Human beings cannot bear too much love. So they turned on him in hatred, and as the nails crashed into His cross, it was almost as though all of us in the cinema were seeing it all for the first time. This is how it had to be. Only out of death do men learn the meaning of life.

At that moment I suddenly found myself thinking of another recent film, a film so different in content and yet saying so very nearly the same thing. In *Who's Afraid of Virginia Woolf?* we had watched a man and woman hating one another because they loved one another, hurting one another to the extent made possible only to those made vulnerable by love. Here was Jesus, utterly vulnerable, taking all the pain, even the pain of feeling forsaken by men and by God, even to the final agony of death, and never once ceasing to love. He gives me the faith that there is no situation in which love cannot be made real, no circumstance which love cannot redeem, no sin which love cannot forgive, no finality beyond the finality of love.

It is not surprising that we find this experience of commitment to Jesus expressed so often in terms not of the intellect but of the heart. Because we are thinking of the Man when we think of Jesus, our relationship with him becomes a personal one, a subjective experience which may be disconnected from any process of human speculation or philosophical quest. It is the breaking in on human life of the awareness that this love shown in Jesus is God's very meaning for our lives. The response to that love calls for a commitment of the believer's whole being.

Kierkegaard describes the encounter in terms of a love affair. He compares the revelation of the divine love to a human courtship, whereby a king would woo a peasant girl. He cannot raise her to his own rank, for this would cause her to cease to be herself. He cannot come to her in all his own splendour, for this would cause her to hide from him. So he chooses to come to her in the form of great humility, seeking equality only with the one he loves.

'Behold where He stands – the God. He is the God, and yet He has not a resting-place for His head and He does not lean on any man lest He cause him to be offended. He is the God, and yet He picks His steps more carefully than if angels guided them, not to prevent His foot from stumbling against a stone, but lest He trample human beings in the dust, in that they are offended in Him. He is the God and yet His eye rests upon mankind with deep concern, for the tender shoots of an individual life may be crushed as easily as a blade of grass. How wonderful a life, all sorrow and all love, to yearn to express the equality of love and yet to be misunderstood; to apprehend the danger that all men may be destroyed and yet only to be able really to save a single soul; his own life filled with sorrow, while each hour of the day is taken up with the troubles of the learner who confides in Him:

This is the God as He stands upon the earth, like unto the humblest by the power of His omnipotent love.'[1]

To accept this kind of love as the ultimate good is to be let in on a new understanding of what life is all about. 'Goodness' is not just a matter of right but of love, and love makes itself known not in power but in humility. The gracious God who comes to me in Jesus comes to me too in the ones whom I serve for his sake. So when I say that I believe that it is he who will come to be the Judge, I mean that he confronts me constantly in all who need my love. His final judgment will be based not on what I have believed but on how much I have loved, and expressed that love in the very deeds of Christ himself:

'Come, blessed of my Father, inherit the kingdom prepared for you from the foundation of the world; for I was hungry and you gave me food, I was thirsty and you gave me drink, I was a stranger and you welcomed me, I was naked and you clothed me, I was sick and you visited me, I was in prison and you came to me . . . as you did it to one of the least of these my brethren, you did it to me.' (Matthew 25:31-46)

So this Man Jesus opens up to all men the possibility of knowing that the perfection of life is love and illuminates that knowledge for us by his own life of love.

But how can that love become a possibility for the essentially egotistical creatures that we are? How can we be switched from our self-centred orbit into a love-centred one? Here again I have to resort to words which express what has been the experience of Christians throughout the centuries. I have to say, again in the words of the Creed, 'I believe in the Holy Spirit'. And when I say that, I mean that I believe that there is a dynamism available to me and to all men that can, as it were, draw us out of one orbit into the other, giving us a new centre and a new energy and a new enthusiasm to make sense out of our lives by working them out in a relationship of love to other people and to God.

Again, I realize that to speak of the Holy Spirit is to speak of a mystery which I cannot explain but which I seem to experience.

---

[1] *Philosophical Fragments:* Kierkegaard.

I experience it in any kind of prompting towards goodness and love. It suggests to me that if there is anything good or purposeful or loving that I feel I ought to do, then the power is there for me to do it if I really try.

We are promised that this same Holy Spirit is to be our Guide, leading us into all truth. I can only say that this seems to echo my own experience that so often in the course of our lives, in our own search for truth, the initiative seems to come from beyond our-selves, so that there are times when we feel as though we are not really as entirely free as we imagined ourselves to be. There are subjective experiences which are very real to us, and on which so many important decisions depend, which we describe in terms that suggest that we are the objects rather than the subjects of them. We speak of 'being called' to some career, of 'falling in love' with some person, of 'receiving' some new idea, of 'being inspired' towards some course of action, of 'discovering' a new truth.

Even in the course of events as they happen we are aware that we are not entirely free to choose which way they will go. There are the things that take us by surprise but which later seem so often to be part of a design. There are the apparent coincidences that prove to have a significance for the subsequent course of our whole lives. A friend, who most of her life was an agnostic, said towards the end of her days, not long before she died of cancer, that she began to believe that God was a real and living Person when she realized how in life's story he 'kept things up His sleeve'. Only a Person would do that.

In fleeting and spasmodic ways I am aware of that kind of per-sonal pressure operating upon and within my own life. It is not that I am constantly aware of the presence of God – most of the time I am not aware of him at all; nor that I know what he wants me to do – usually when I have to make decisions I feel that I have not a clue as to which is the 'right' decision to make. But I can never get away from the feeling that even though I am not aware of him, he somehow is aware of me and that he knows, even in a personal way, where I am and what I am about and what it would be best for me to do. So I find myself compelled to agree that

'There is a divinity that shapes our ends
Rough-hew them as we will.'

But if this is a personal divinity, then it must be possible for men
to have personal communication with him. I find that the most
meaningful kind of communication with God is that which I share
in community with others. This is why corporate worship and the
life of a Christian community are so important to me. But there
are dangers, even in the life of community, lest we deceive ourselves and demand of other people that they be other than they
are. Bonheffer, writing about the experience of life with other
Christians, reminds us:

'Just as surely as God desires to lead us to a knowledge of
genuine Christian fellowship, so surely must we be overwhelmed
by a great disillusionment with others, with Christians in general,
and, if we are fortunate, with ourselves.'[1]

It is only in a realism that enables us to accept one another as we
really are, so that we are prepared to let each other be, that we too
can fully accept ourselves and the meaning of our own being
in communication with its Source.

The experience of corporate worship can bring to the whole
of life a splendid fourth dimension. Even the meanest of chapels
and the smallest of congreagations can on occasion experience it.
I feel as though I know well the experience which John Betjeman
describes in *Undenominational* as he sees the lone chapel in the
country lane, its walls shaking to the sound of its hymns:

'Revival ran along the hedge
And made my spirit whole,
When steam was on the window panes
And glory in my soul.'[2]

But this kind of revival of spirit becomes most meaningful when
the company of people have gathered expressly for communion
together, linked backwards through the past to the life of Jesus
himself as they share the symbols of his last supper, and linked

[1] *Life Together*, Dietrich Bonhoeffer, SCM Press.
[2] *Collected Poems:* John Betjeman, pub. John Murray.

forwards through to the future as they look to that which is beyond the limits of death and time and place to the hope of his coming again. For me this became most real in the genuine Christian community whose life I was privileged to share for a short time at East Harlem. This congregation transcended the barriers of race and sex and class, and had become a company in which people really were trying to share a common life and to give reality to the expression of the love in which they believed. When they worshipped together, the sense of the presence of God would on occasions be so overwhelmingly real that the whole celebration became more like a wedding feast with the Bridegroom present than like a solemn religious service.

At East Harlem, as at all places of authentic Christian community, the Spirit who was so evidently present when the congregation came together was the same Spirit who was recognized to be active in the purposeful events that were shaping the life of their whole community. They believed that he called them to be present with him in all the key struggles of society, in all the striving after justice and harmony and peace, in every attempt to open up to all men the possibility of realizing their full humanity. So the deeds they were called upon to act out among men were the deeds of Christ himself, and they had no doubt that they would be given the energy and the power and the love to do them. For them, faith was an experience that worked, and it worked by love.

Faith and hope and love, St Paul tells us, are all closely intertwined. Certainly when faith fades, hope seems to fade also. But faith is more than mere hoping against hope that these things might be so. It is a decision, and the very word 'decision' means the cutting off of all other possibilities. We decide by faith that there is a meaning in our lives, that there is an ultimate choice to be made freely and that the choice is directed to the love revealed to us through the Being of one perfect Man. The decision has to be made in darkness but it can be lived out in light. And even when faith fails and our hope grows dim, there remains always the possibility of love. This, for me, in the final analysis, is what it means to believe in God.

GEORGE ALLEN & UNWIN LTD
London: 40 Museum Street, W.C.1.

Auckland: P.O. Box 36013, Northcote Central. N.4
Barbados: P.O. Box 222, Bridgetown
Beirut: Deep Building, Jeanne d'Arc Street
Bombay: 15 Graham Road, Ballard Estate, Bombay 1
Buenos Aires: Escritorio 454-459, Florida 165
Calcutta: 17 Chittaranjan Avenue, Calcutta 13
Cape Town: 68 Shortmarket Street
Hong Kong: 105 Wing On Mansion, 26 Hancow Road, Kowloon
Ibadan: P.O. Box 62
Karachi: Karachi Chambers, McLeod Road
Madras: Mohan Mansions, 38c Mount Road, Madras 6
Mexico: Villalongin 32-10, Piso, Mexico 5, D.F.
Nairobi: P.O. Box 4536
New Delhi: 13-14 Asaf Ali Road, New Delhi 1
Ontario: 81 Curlew Drive, Don Mills
Philippines: Manila P.O. Box 4432
Rio de Janeiro: Caixa Postal 2537-Zc-00
Sao Paulo: Caixa Postal 8675
Singapore: 36c Prinsep Street, Singapore 7
Sydney, N.S.W.: Bradbury House, 55 York Street
Tokyo: P.O. Box 26, Kamata

I Believe

W. H. AUDEN, PEARL BUCK, E. M. FORSTER, HAVELOCK ELLIS, LANCELOT HOGBEN, THOMAS MANN, BERTRAND RUSSELL, H. G. WELLS, REBECCA WEST and others.

Here, in all its exciting diversity, is the inner voice of our age, the private counterpart to its public controversies. The contributors to this book are all distinguished men and women of the past fifty years; some have written of the ideas that have sustained them, or for which they have stood; some have described the view of life their experience has shaped; and some, more personal have made individual affirmations of faith in the human spirit. To read them today, with all their differences of outlook, nationality and calling, European, American and Chinese, poet, humorist and scientist, Catholic and Communist, is a heartening reminder of the cultural riches that can spring from intellectual freedom, tolerance and goodwill.

What I Believe

A. J. AYER, KENNETH C. BARNES, LORD BOOTHBY, JOHN BRATBY, ARTHUR CALDER-MARSHALL, MARGARET COLE, DAPHNE DU MAURIER, EDWARD GLOVER, ROSEMARY HAUGHTON, JACQUETTA HAWKES, MALCOLM MUGGER-IDGE, KATHLEEN NOTT, J. B. PRIESTLEY, EDWARD G. SLESINGER, NORMAN ST JOHN-STEVAS, MERVYN STOCKWOOD, BARBARA WOOTTON, JOHN WREN-LEWIS.

What *do* you believe? About life, about its purposes? In this age of scepticism the question is probably asked more restlessly and answered more tentatively than ever before. Here, some of the liveliest minds of today give their particular answers. Some of the most interesting, in personal vein, affirm their faith in the human spirit, in life-enhancing activity, others, including a distinguished surgeon, see their lives in terms of service, or are more directly concerned with current social questions. An artist, whose work is his belief, makes a strong stand for the individual, a well-known public figure, for robust good-fellowship. And within more clearly labelled frameworks there are cogent humanist statements as well as several remarkable contributions by Christians, orthodox and un-orthodox, who view the perennial truths of their faith through modern eyes. The book becomes, as one reads it, a growing revelation of how men and women find meaning in life and successfully 'challenge and dominate the shameless dark'.

This is My Philosophy

BERTRAND RUSSELL, ALDOUS HUXLEY, JEAN-PAUL SARTRE, ALBERT SCHWEITZER, G. M. TREVELYAN, CARL JUNG, S. RADHAKRISHNAN, JACQUES MARITAN and others.

Each selection in this book is a statement of personal philosophy by one of the world's leading thinkers. The contributors are twenty eminent living philosophers, scientists, statesmen, authors, historians, educators, sociologists, and theologians. Each has selected from his own writings (or has written especially for this book) an expression of his approach to life, his work, and our present-day world.

Here are the matured reflections of men who have lived a full and busy life and have achieved wisdom with their years. What is man's relation to the world today? To history? To society? To death? To God? To country? What is thinking? What is our civilization coming to? Can the East and West find a philosophy of life in common? How does the Christian ethic stand up in an atom-splitting world? What is mankind's greatest present need?

These are some of the questions treated in a book of many points of view; a challenging collection of seasoned reflections on the biggest and most fundamental problems, conflicts, and concepts of man to-day.

Masterpieces of World Philosophy

EDITED BY FRANK N. MAGILL   ASSOCIATE EDITOR: IAN P. MCGREAL

Distilled in this enormous volume is the wisdom of the ages, the key thinking of the world's greatest philosophers. For students and thoughtful readers and as a reference, it offers a rich treasure. Two hundred vastly influential philosophical works by 139 different thinkers are summarized. Some of these men of the ages are represented by one central book which gives the essence of their systematized thought. Others are represented by a number of works—Plato by seventeen, Aristotle by eight, Kant by three.

Each analysis, presented in essay review of around 3,000 or more words, provides a strictly factual appraisal of the essence of the monumental work. At the beginning of each is valuable reference data—the type of work, the dates of the author's birth and death, and of the work itself, and a few sentences which state the principal ideas advanced. The text of the summaries is set in double columns for easy reading. At the back is a glossary of philosophical terms.

The Genesis of Twentieth Century Philosophy

HARRY PROSCH

Dr Prosch takes us back to Copernicus and lucidly explains exactly what is meant by 'the Copernican Revolution'. Then we move forward with him through the responses of Copernicus and the new insights added by such men as Kepler, Galileo, and Newton. He makes clear what Descartes was trying to say, and Hobbes, Locke, Berkley, Hume, Kant, Hegel and many more.

Dr Prosch shows that if we are acquainted with the problems and terminology of these men, we are well prepared to understand the four schools of modern philosophy: the pragmatists, the Marxists, the logical analysts, and the existentialists of today. Dr Prosch's books does a serious job with great good humour and marvellous clarity; the willing and alert reader can come away from it with a grasp of the heritage and preoccupation of the most powerful minds of our civilization.

History of Western Philosophy

BERTRAND RUSSELL

'It is certain of a very wide audience, and is, in my opinion, just the kind of thing people ought to have to make them understand the past. . . . It may be one of the most valuable books of our time.'

G. M. TREVELYAN

'Bertrand Russell's remarkable book is, so far as I am aware, the first attempt to present a history of western philosophy in relation to its social and economic background. As such, and also as a brilliantly written exposé of changing philosophical doctrines, it should be widely read.'

JULIAN HUXLEY

'A survey of western philosophy in relation to its environment, of such sweep and acuteness, alive in every nerve, is a masterpiece of intellectual energy . . . the Socrates of our time.'

A. L. ROWSE

Men Seeking God

CHRISTOPHER MAYHEW M.P.

Christopher Mayhew's outstandingly successful series of television pro-
grammes, 'Men Seeking God,' gave rise to this sincere effort to present
the great religions of the world. The book describes the faith of a number
of devout and representative adherents of these religions—Swami Lokes-
warananda, a Hindu monk who runs a hostel for poor students in the
slums of Calcutta; U San Nyun, a Buddhist layman, living near Rangoon;
the Rev. Isaac Levy, Rabbi of the Hampstead Synagogue; Mulauna
Muhammad Ali, a Moslem prayer leader living in Lahore; Father
Germanus, a Franciscan friar, and the Rev. C. C. Pande, an Indian
Methodist minister who supervises a leper colony in Bengal. Each person
explains his conception of God, his methods of prayer and worship, and
his idea of man's destiny; and gives a selection of his favourite Scriptural
quotations. In the concluding chapter Mr. Mayhew attempts a summing
up. The book contains a large number of striking photographs.

God is my Adventure

ROM LANDAU

Few men have searched more open-heartedly for spiritual truth than
Rom Landau; and that is the appeal of his book. When it first appeared
in 1935 (and became an immediate best-seller) it gave the ordinary reader
a rare insight into the movements and leaders of the inter-war years.
The formidable Ouspensky, the mysterious Gurdjieff, Frank Buchman
and the Oxford Group (now Moral Rearmament), Rudolf Steiner, the
founder of anthroposophy, Krishnamurti, the golden boy of the theosopists
—Rom Landau met them all, and others ready always to take in the new
message, feel the impact of strong, and strange, personalities, and ready
also, his critical faculties undimmed, to sense the bogus and the preten-
tious. A postscript specially written for this edition brings it up to date
and completes an unusual view of Europe's unfolding inner life.

Vedanta for Modern Man

CHRISTOPHER ISHERWOOD

This is an excellent introduction to a system of religion which views all faiths as of value and encourages the study of all as the first step towards genuine enlightenment. It is an anthology, rich in variety and learning, and it follows the pattern of the successful *Vedanta for the Western World*. Separate phases of the philosophy and technique of Vedanta—the divine nature of man, the Godward purpose of life, and the essential unity of all religions—are treated in 61 chapters. These also include essays on related subjects, such as art and religion, religion and the world crisis, the religious novel, notes on personalities such as William Law, Emerson and Sri Ramakrishna and some poetry selections. All have previously appeared as material in a magazine *Vedanta and the West*.

Vedanta for the Western World

EDITED AND INTRODUCED BY CHRISTOPHER ISHERWOOD

Vedanta is the wisdom of the Vedas, the perennial philosophy distilled over centuries in India from the oldest known religious writings. It is in fact the philosophy underlying all religion. Here, a vigorous group of writers in California, inspired by the Ramakrishna Mission, examine different aspects of it for the benefit of the West. Aldous Huxley, Gerald Heard, and Christopher Isherwood, amongst others, write on the true nature of yoga, the reality of man's divinity, the methods by which we can all realize ourselves, and the intimate connection between Christianity and Vedanta. In their own personal search for a faith they have gone to the fountainhead, and have found there the larger, more universal, 'religion of man' that the world needs today.

GEORGE ALLEN & UNWIN LTD